COMPASSION

A journey through love, loss and understanding of mental illness

—

Hayden Fricke
Brother, Son, Psychologist

Dedications

I dedicate this book to Quentin, Craig, Glenn and Dad - four men in my life who struggled with different types of mental illness – and all the other people in the world who have either experienced mental illness themselves or have cared for those who are suffering. I hope we can all learn to understand and build more compassion.

"Compassion is not a virtue – it is a commitment. Its' not something we have or don't have – it's something we choose to practice."

Brené Brown

Contents

Introduction	1
An Episode to Begin	4
Earliest Memories	9
Q's Teenage Years	12
Craig – my life is difficult too	19
Reflections on historical changes in parenting	26
Nana – it's in the family	29
Why is it hard to talk about mental illness?	34
Family breakdown – divorce and chaos	37
Divorce and the Impact on Children	43
Dad – alcoholism and bipolar disorder	45
Reflecting on my father	52
Q – Break-down #1	55
Diagnosis and the early years	59
Understanding Schizophrenia	60
Episodes	65
Schizophrenia and cigarettes	68
Can things get any worse?	70
Conversations with people with mental illness	77

Long-term patterns	79
The psychiatric system	83
Wheelchair Tennis	86
Meaning, purpose and empathy	89
Israel	91
Mental illness and human rights	97
Delusions and Hallucinations	99
The mental health system	102
Back to Craig – don't forget me	112
A qualification to parent, and support for those who struggle	118
Glenn – Spiralling down	120
The impact on Yvette's family	131
The last few years with Q	136
Back to Craig and what's happening now	148
Housing, financial capacity and ageing	153
How has this shaped me personally and professionally?	155
How have these experiences informed my work?	165
How has this shaped the people around me?	168
What have I learnt from these experiences? What has helped me?	179
What else should we do as a society?	183
Acknowledgements	187
About Hayden	190

Introduction

This book is about my 37-year personal journey, the mental illness in my family, and my reflections as a psychologist on these experiences. Whilst many of the events were tragic and harrowing, I feel the need to share them so that people facing similar challenges know that they are not alone. Mental illness has impacted my life and that of those around me in obvious ways and, furthermore, as a psychologist I have some insights into the stories from a broader societal perspective.

I decided to call the book *Compassion*, because my aim is to increase awareness and understanding of the different forms of mental illness in the hope that this leads to less stigma and more compassion across Australia.

We frequently lump a wide range of mental health conditions under the one heading of 'mental illness', however different types of mental illness may affect individuals and families in divergent ways. For example, my brother Q had schizophrenia, which is repeatedly misunderstood. I will explain this illness in more detail later, but essentially it is where a person's mind is extremely mixed up, typically distorted and somewhat delusional in nature. Schizophrenia can be an extremely complicated illness that manifests in different ways. In my family, our experience of schizophrenia was regularly traumatic and often sad.

This is unlike my memory of my father, who was highly successful as a lawyer, barrister, QC, and judge, yet who struggled with bipolar disorder and alcoholism. Most of my memories of my father are not traumatic like those of my brother Q, but they are sometimes frustrating and at times confusing and hard to comprehend.

My brother Craig has had a different series of challenges. He is the only one of the four main people in my story still alive today. His life makes me believe that some form of struggle and suffering is normal. Life is not always a perfect Instagram post, and in fact Craig's life has lacked these moments. His intellectual disability, combined with anxiety and depression, has made many aspects more difficult, but he has been resilient and, at the moment, his life at the age of 61 is perhaps the most positive it has ever been.

The final story is about my brother-in-law Glenn, whose condition gradually deteriorated as his clinical depression spiralled downwards and eventually led to him taking his own life. Pure sadness and grief are the main emotions I feel for him.

I want to share these different stories about four people close to me who each had a profound influence on my life to explain how much mental illnesses may differ. I imagine that most of you will be able to understand and empathise with at least one case. Given that mental illness is so common, most readers will have either experienced it themselves, lived it through family members, or at least know someone with a mental illness. Therefore, these stories and my reflections and insights will be relevant to almost all readers.

Beyond relating my personal stories, the broader perspectives I can provide as a psychologist help to focus on exactly what the different mental illnesses are on a higher level of understanding, how they transformed me and my family, and what some of the societal issues are in relation to how we tend to deal with them. By telling my own story and explaining the psychological perspective, I aim to increase your understanding and compassion for those with a mental illness, as well as the conversations we have on this challenging topic.

Medications for mental illness improve continually. They are more effective now at reducing some of the negative impacts of illnesses, and their side effects are being managed better and are less severe than they used to be. We don't lock people away in 'mental asylums' anymore, and there are countless examples of how we have improved the treatment and management of mental illness in our society. However, we still have a very long way to go in terms of our conversations about this complex issue.

Groups like R U OK? that promote better conversations have been wonderful, but we need to build on this and go further and deeper. I would really love to see a positive shift in conversations in homes and in workplaces across Australia. After we have asked others if they are OK, I would be incredibly extremely pleased if many more people knew what to do next. We do not have to treat them, but we all need to learn some micro-skills – how to ask good open questions to encourage people to talk about themselves, and skills in:

- listening without judging or trying to solve problems
- showing empathy and compassion
- finding small ways to help support people with mental illnesses and helping to reduce their suffering just a little bit as well as enhancing the quality of their lives in tiny but critical ways.

Many people don't feel comfortable with these conversations or have confidence in their own ability to conduct them without feeling awkward or uneasy. Stigma is still strong in our society, but it is only through learning to talk about it more frequently that we will shift the dial and make a positive difference to those living with a mental illness. I hope this book helps you develop some of these conversational skills and gain a better understanding.

A note of caution

This book is very real, raw, and often traumatic. If it triggers strong negative emotions, you may want to talk with professionals. Furthermore, if you find yourself facing mental health difficulties, or if a loved one is experiencing problems, it's important to know that you're not alone and can contact any of the following organisations for help and support:

- SANE Australia: https://www.sane.org/
- The Blue Knot Helpline and Redress Support Service: https://blueknot.org.au/
- Beyond Blue: https://lnkd.in/gPFwFvE4
- Lifeline: https://lnkd.in/g4KW4HmF
- Mindspot: https://lnkd.in/gH7zbG5E

An Episode to Begin

This is my recollection of what ought to have been a perfectly normal long weekend in November 1986 in a suburban house of an ordinary Australian family. Recollections of events long since faded are typically vague, edited by time and largely forgotten, but something so inexplicable, so bewildering and painful happened that day that it remains etched in my memory with a painful clarity that remains hard to talk about.

I am one of Mum (Judy) and Dad (Graham)'s four children. Craig is the eldest brother. He is a little over three years older than me, and Quentin was two years younger. My parents finally got their wish for a girl when my sister Yvette was born two years after Quentin. We lived in Brighton, a wealthy suburb by the beach in Melbourne. My siblings and I were fortunate to have grown up in a large house with a tennis court and swimming pool in our backyard, but although we lived in a wealthy area, we did not have a lavish lifestyle. Our family home was nice, but not newly decorated or extravagant in any way.

Mum and Yvette, who was 15 years old at this time, were away. They had been staying with friends at a farm in Gippsland, and on their way home they stopped in at long-time friends of the family in Narre Warren North. My younger brother Quentin and I were at home by ourselves for the weekend. Q, as we had called Quentin since he was little, was 17. I was 19 and had recently returned from 12 months in the US, having taken up a tennis scholarship at a college in Tennessee, and I had begun to play the world tennis satellite circuit.

Q was also playing tennis full-time. He had been exceptional as a junior with more talent and dedication than me and won many junior tennis tournaments in Victoria and around Australia. He was a little taller than I was at just under six feet and had a lean and athletic build. Q was a baseliner with such patience and determination that playing him was like hitting against a brick wall; he rarely missed.

A few months prior to the long weekend at home, he had been playing a series of tennis tournaments in Spain. Before I went to the US, I used to organise everything for him when we travelled, but this time I was not available to help, and he had to manage by himself. He was a young 17-year-old on his own in a foreign country and struggling to cope with it all. The pressure built up to a point where he had a 'nervous breakdown' and returned home. He had been struggling since then, and his tennis had gone downhill rapidly, as had many other aspects of his life. My family didn't know much about mental illness back then, and we didn't have the words to describe what was happening, but we knew something wasn't quite right.

I came home on the Monday afternoon of the long weekend. I can't recall where I had been. I walked in the side entrance and on through the laundry door which led into the family kitchen, and my jaw dropped as I saw the laundry cupboards had been smashed beyond recognition. My mind began racing. The fervour and force of the blows that must have caused this damage were clearly enormous. But who had done this? I walked on through to the kitchen, my heart pounding, taking in the destruction of what seemed like every surface and appliance. As I made my way through the entire house, the absolute shock of it all hit me when I realised with disbelief that our whole home had been shattered. Doors hung off their hinges and a large light in the living room dangled pathetically near the ground, having been pulled out of its socket in the ceiling. It was as if a tornado has gone through our home. Debris was all over the floor as I made my way through each room. Windows were demolished, furniture broken, walls bashed in. It was too much to comprehend in a place where I had always felt safe. Most of the house was ruined. Where was Q?

My mind was unable to process what I was witnessing, and my body later went into a state of total shock. After I had walked through each room, I realised that my brother was responsible, but I could not comprehend how twisted his mind must have been or how much force had been required over a sustained period to carry out the destruction of our home with such passion. Q and I had always been very close: we were born two years apart, and we had spent countless hours on the tennis court together. I just knew that something must have snapped in his brain.

Q had used an axe to destroy our home, which he believed was too materialistic. He later told Mum that everything worldly and money-oriented needed to be demolished, and that he was "destroying our idols." In his mind he had freed our home of its demons.

At that moment, all alone looking at all the wrecked rooms, I tried to make sense of it all, but I couldn't. I had summoned all that I had at this point, but then collapsed onto the floor. In a dazed state, I crawled to the corner of the room, where I found the bottom of a curtain next to our piano, and I curled myself into a ball and wrapped myself in the curtain. I cried uncontrollably. I shook. I was on the edge of losing it myself. I stayed in that foetal position for over an hour, rocking back and forth, unable to move. My mind was distorted. I wondered if I was having a breakdown myself. It was incomprehensible that the brother I had grown up with, shared a room with, shared a bunk bed with for years, played tennis with forever, and whom I loved, was capable of this. Mum and Yvette arrived home and found me like this. With concern and compassion, they helped me to eventually pull myself together enough to get up and begin making some sense of it all.

Q was clearly troubled and tortured, and unable to think clearly. He had run away immediately after destroying the house. Whatever triggered his assault on our home had created an equal desire to run from it. He had tried to catch a train to Sydney without a ticket, money, or even a purpose. Mum called the police, and not long afterwards they found him. This wasn't too difficult given that he was wild-eyed, dishevelled and, for some unknown reason, he was also half-naked. Mum drove to Brighton Police Station, where a police psychiatrist had him certified. I didn't know what this meant at the time, but I now understand he was certified as being unable to take care of his own health and safety. Essentially, his right to take care of himself was taken away, and the government was now responsible for him.

The police took Q in a divisional panel wagon, known at the time as a 'divvy van' to Larundel Mental Asylum, and Mum followed in her car. This was his first visit to that terrible place. At the beginning of World War II in 1939, Larundel was built to replace the Kew Asylum. Even the name asylum attests to the type of place it was. It was part of a larger mental health complex known as Mont Park, and famous for housing some of the most severely mentally ill criminals in Australia. It was closed in 1999. Sadly, Q was hospitalised at Larundel for many months on that first occasion.

In those less enlightened times, the main form of help on offer to patients (or were they referred to as inmates?) was a very high dose of drugs - some to sedate them (lithium), some to reduce any psychotic symptoms (olanzapine or haloperidol), and others to help cope with their side effects (Cogentin).

I vividly remember my first visit to Larundel shortly after Q was admitted. I walked through the entrance, and my first and lasting impression was of the oversized, heavy, and unwelcoming door that closed with a thud and imparted to all who entered "you won't leave here anytime soon." Inside, patients were walking around, and I was stunned by how hopeless and dishevelled they looked. When I saw Q, like all the other patients he was medicated to the eyeballs. He walked like a robot with stiff limbs, his face devoid of emotion, and his eyes staring straight ahead or down at the floor as he shuffled along. On other visits he was in a catatonic state – awake, but not responsive to other people or his environment. All I could do was sit quietly with him.

Larundel also had a positive side. The staff were kind and caring to Q, and they were thoughtful in their interactions with Mum. There were some freedoms for Q too. Mum recalls taking him for lovely walks in the wonderful parklands and gardens at Larundel. Once she took him out to a game of tennis at Festival Hall, where they watched Pat Cash play. In this way, he had some level of independence and was able to go out into the world as long as it was safe.

This episode took place over 37 years ago and was a most challenging experience for everyone in our family and our close friends. New emotions, drugs, institutions, sadness, even moments of laughter shone through at times, although these were largely muffled by a confused story that none of us understood. It was all new to us. No doubt Q struggled to understand what was happening to him as well. He was going through such trauma. It all happened so fast and without warning.

While he was always an unusual and quirky kid, he had never been disturbed and delusional like this. Something in his brain had snapped. Mum, Yvette and I were all trying to comprehend what was happening. In these moments it is only human to cry out for meaning and a diagnosis, but this was the first time we had heard the term schizophrenia and at the time we didn't know what it was, nor what it meant. One doctor told us sadly it was like a "death sentence". Our family has never forgotten his comment. It was extremely unhelpful and brutal. Schizophrenia is not a death sentence, although Q did lead a very sad life.

Everyone did their best to help him live a reasonable life, and he did manage to have fun and enjoyment between the sad and disturbing periods. This book tells his story so that you will understand what I'm talking about.

Earliest Memories

Q was born on 4 March 1969. My mum was a typical wife of the times and took care of the house and raised the children. I remember her responding to a question about her occupation and writing down 'home duties'. She excelled at these, and created a healthy environment for us to grow up in. Dad was a barrister, then Queen's Counsel, then later a judge in the County Court of Victoria. The County Court hears an infinite variety of cases from theft up to intentionally causing serious injury, but more serious crimes such as murders are dealt with in the Supreme Court of Victoria. Dad was the provider for our family, and he did this very well. As children we never wanted for anything.

Q was almost exactly two years younger than me. He struggled to say the name Yvette when he was little, and so he called her Bettie, and he ended up calling her Bettie for the rest of his life. Yvette as a young toddler couldn't say Q, and she called him Ken-Ken. It was always cute to listen to them referring to each other as Bettie and Ken-Ken.

My earliest memories of Q are that he was always a very happy, smiling, funny, quirky kid. He had this cheeky grin on his face that I can still see today, and he would delight in getting up to mischief and finding the fun in small daily activities. For as long as I can recall, Q and I shared a bedroom. We slept in bunk beds with Q on the top and me on the bottom, and we would talk to each other in bed at night as we fell asleep. Yvette told us that she would regularly hear us, but she knew we were asleep, so we must have unconsciously developed a habit of talking as we went to sleep and even during the early parts of our sleep, possibly in a semi-conscious state. We were different from each other, but we were close, and we got on together very well.

Q had great energy. Now that I have my own son, I realise this is not uncommon, and in fact most mothers would probably say this about their boys. As a father of two girls as well, I am aware that girls tend to be more calm, gentle, and placid at a younger age. Having said this, Mum had two boys prior to Q, and he was energetic on another level. When he was about nine years old, Mum took him to see a psychiatrist, who diagnosed a hyperactivity disorder. Q was no longer allowed sugary lollies and was taken off everything with processed sugar, which included something known as salicylate. Even apples were off the menu for Q, and the psychiatrist gave him exercises to do each day. They seem quite strange, looking back: he had to crawl using the opposite technique to the way you normally would. That is, you normally move your left arm and right leg together, but he was required to move the left arm and left leg at the same time. I'm not quite sure how this connected to his hyperactivity, but he did have co-ordination problems, and it seemed to help. In his early years, Q played many sports, and one was Australian Rules Football, where he was told he had two left feet. My mother understood this, but also knew that nobody tried harder than Q when he set his mind on something.

In addition to the strange exercises Q had to do daily, he was put on a calming drug called methylphenidate, a medication now commonly used to treat attention deficit hyperactivity disorder (ADHD). At the time, in the mid- to late-1970s, ADHD wasn't as prevalent as it is today, and in fact, it was originally called hyperkinetic reaction of childhood. It wasn't until the 1960s that the American Psychiatric Association formally recognised it as a mental disorder, and in the 1980s it became 'attention deficit disorder with or without hyperactivity'. Q struggled to sit still at school and was easily distracted, looking around for something silly to do. This clearly didn't help him concentrate and study in class. Mum gave him one methylphenidate tablet each morning before school, which helped him concentrate a little better.

Sometimes his hyperactivity got him into trouble. I remember one occasion when he was about seven, and at Narre Warren North primary school. It must have been recess, because he was running around the classroom when he tripped and fell. Although I wasn't there, I can clearly imagine this part in slow motion. As he was falling, his head went straight into the corner of a table. He didn't have time to put his hands out and so his mouth and front teeth hit the table. One of his front teeth was almost knocked out, left dangling from a thread, and his mouth bled profusely. Once he was cleaned up and the bleeding stopped, he was taken to the dentist for emergency treatment. The dentist was able to put his tooth back, but unfortunately the nerve had died, and it turned black over the next few weeks. The other children all teased him and called him "dead tooth", which he hated.

When Q was about eight years old, he became obsessed with all the superheroes on television and in comic books. In particular, he loved Superman. He wanted to be Superman. He wanted to fly like Superman. Thinking this was a young boy's normal dream, Mum made him a Superman cape. Mum had her own sewing machine, and Q watched in anticipation as she set about making it.

Q loved it. It clearly had Superman powers. He was meticulous in his preparations to fly, running around the house with arms stretched out, practising his moves and exploring whether to use his obvious powers for good or evil. We lived on a large seven-acre property in Narre Warren at that time - the perfect test pad for his impending launch and with plenty of room for Q to stretch his wings. He had options with several tall trees, but chose the house, climbing up onto the roof of our 1970's single-storey home. Mum was busy as she was permanently, just happy that the kids were outside, but Craig was witness to the impending challenge - Q versus gravity - and suddenly his voice cut through the sounds of suburban bliss. "Mum! Quentin is going to jump off the roof!" "Catch him!" she shrieked in reply - surprise, desperation and disbelief in equal measure in her voice. Q's maiden voyage was away as he leapt into the great unknown perhaps, although for him the trajectory of his take-off suggested far greater certainty. He leapt outwards and upwards, his legs trailing behind as his landing gear was clearly not going to be required for some time. His arms were stretched forward, his whole body was parallel to the ground with the confidence of a superhero, and Craig, who was just 13 at the time, followed Mum's anguished plea, positioned himself under Q with a split-second to spare, and caught him. It was good that Mum was there to witness the failure of her cape. Q was shattered - physically unhurt, but psychologically wounded by the realisation that flight was beyond him.

Q's Teenage Years

Our older brother Craig was outstanding at many sports. He was larger and stronger than most kids until his late teenage years, and he loved Australian Rules Football. I remember watching him play in one game when he was about 12 years old, and he kicked ten goals. This is an amazing feat at any level of football. He stood tall, and each time the ball came down to the forward line he outmanoeuvred his smaller opposition to mark the ball (or 'catch' in non-football language). He was also a strong tennis player and had a powerful serve and a hard-hitting forehand. Swimming was another sport he excelled at. He had broad, powerful shoulders, and was more accomplished than most swimmers of his age. Mum used to take us all to the Doveton swimming pool twice each week. We loved the Friday evening swimming sessions, because we knew that afterwards we would be treated to fish and chips for dinner.

I was also good at sport, although not nearly as strong or as talented as Craig. I was a reasonably good swimmer, but my best sports were tennis and snow skiing. We spent about a month up at Mt Buller each winter, skiing all day, every day. I was in skiing squads, competed in regular races, and just loved the environment up at the snow. Tennis was an all-year-round sport though, and I started to excel early. No doubt the fact that we had a tennis court in our backyard made a difference. Mum and Dad both played tennis and loved the sport, however they had not played as children and only took it up in their thirties when they could afford their own tennis court. I used to hit balls with Mum and Dad, and I had tennis lessons from the age of about six. I recall the first time I was able to beat Dad in a game of singles - I was only ten years old and was

Q – dressed up for a wedding and smiling during better times as a young adult

playing with a broken left arm in a cast. As a right-handed player it didn't hamper me much, and I beat Dad in a very close and tight match 6-5 in a set. I never lost to my father again after that.

I also loved horse riding. We had a white horse called Snow - how original! Notwithstanding that, I should say that Snow rarely looked very white because he frequently rolled in mud and was quite dirty until we spent enough time brushing him, which was not often enough. I had riding lessons from Dianne Luc, who was the mother of Yvette's best friend, Michelle. She taught me how to jump over small logs and other obstacles. One day Craig, Q and I decided (stupidly) to try to ride Snow. That would normally have been fine if we did it one at a time, but we thought we would try without a bridle or saddle, and with all three of us on his back at once. We were kids and except for Craig we didn't weigh a lot, but Snow was not a large horse. He didn't appreciate our efforts and proceeded to kick and buck, so we all fell off. We deserved this, and never tried it again.

Another time, Q had been riding Snow around our paddock. We were casual with Snow and treated him more like a pet. This time Q must have taken Snow out of the paddock and into an area near our home that was not fenced off. I don't remember the full story, but Q must have wanted to go home to get something. He rode up to the house and tied Snow up while he went inside, however, he didn't choose a very good hitching post: a small three-wheeler tricycle. Snow was spooked by something and ran off with his reins tied to the tricycle. Somehow it didn't end up in tragedy for Snow or Q, but this was the type of thing Q did regularly without thinking.

With two older brothers who loved a variety of sports, it was not surprising that Q wanted to copy us. However, he was more challenged as an athlete because of his co-ordination problems. He struggled with the intricate skills of football and simply could not match Craig's ability, or mine in the pool as he found it hard to put his head in the water and breath properly. However, his early aptitude for tennis showed real potential. As young kids living on a farm, we often got bored and since we had a tennis court in our backyard we would play regularly. When you combine this with Q's steely determination, he began to excel at tennis around the age of ten or 11. We moved from Narre Warren North to Brighton when Q was nine, and we were lucky the house had room for a court and Mum and Dad had one built shortly after we arrived there. As kids we loved the country with its space and freedoms, and we all cried when we were told we were moving to Brighton. We didn't know where it was, but I remember being extremely upset that we would no longer be able to ride horses or run around in the open. I had images of confined spaces and concrete areas without green grass. Later I would love Brighton, particularly for its beaches, but initially we didn't have many friends or things to do, and so Q and I played tennis together for hours.

We joined the Brighton Tennis Club and played in junior teams. When I was about 14 and Q was 12, I was quite a bit better than he was, however by the time we were about 16 and 18 Q had caught up. While I loved tennis, I also loved girls and partying, but Q was single-minded and only interested in tennis. He was determined to the point of obsession. It was his life, and his devotion to tennis and passion for it drove him to reach a standard that was beyond his years. He was a baseline player with heavy topspin groundstrokes, including a double-handed backhand. He was like a brick wall, and never missed. At 16 and 17, as Q became taller and stronger, he also developed a lot more power in his shots, and when he combined power and consistency, he won many matches, frequently against older players.

When we were between 12 and 16, Mum took us both to tennis tournaments all over Melbourne, and our trophy cabinet grew. I won many more matches in the earlier years, but Q was certainly catching me up as he matured and improved. I was probably a better doubles player than Q, whereas in his late teens he was becoming a better singles player.

I remember a time when we both played the Brighton Club Championships. It was rare that we played the same events because of our age difference, but this was an open age event. We had both made it through to the final and played each other. Q took the early lead and was beating me reasonably convincingly. I was humiliated at losing to my little brother and must have looked despondent. He picked up on this and told me later that he had felt sorry for me. That was his problem - he let it affect his performance. He dropped off, and I started playing better and eventually beat him.

We both longed to be professional tennis players, and loved watching champions like Bjorn Borg, John McEnroe, Jimmy Connors, and Mats Wilander. Q styled his game on Borg and played quite like him. We both regularly dreamt of playing against these champions and would wake up in the morning and tell each other if we had played a match in our sleep against a superstar. In fact, for me this continued for many years, and early on in our marriage my wife Lynne would ask "So who did you play last night?" For some reason it was usually Pete Sampras. Mum knew that we both wanted to play tennis as a career. I was not doing well at school because I was putting all my passion and energy into tennis, and she told me to study hard enough to pass Year 12 so that I had that as a back-up plan in case I didn't make it to the top of professional tennis. I did manage to pass Year 12, although only just - I failed two out of five subjects. When I finished, I started playing the Satellite Tennis Circuit in Australia and applied for tennis scholarships to colleges in the US. I was fortunate enough to be offered a full tennis scholarship to a college in Tennessee called Freed-Hardeman University, where they paid my food, board, education, and tennis gear. I only had to pay my airfare and spending money for 12 months. Unbeknown to me when I accepted, it was in the middle of the Bible Belt and the college was a devout Church of Christ university. I had finished my Year 12 in November 1984, but the

US school year is different from Australia's, and I wasn't due to begin my college year until September 1985, so I decided to travel around Australia playing tennis until then.

Q was only 16 years old, and he joined me on the circuit. He had just completed Year 10 and had no back-up plan. Q was 100 percent all in on making it as a professional tennis player. He would not consider any other option. Looking back, I struggle to understand how Mum and Dad let him leave school and play tennis full-time so young, travelling without supervision (except me, I suppose). He did manage to work for nine months at Peerless Crumpets, but Mum had to push him daily to turn up. Q wanted to play tennis overseas, and Mum insisted he work to pay for it. I must admit that we did have some amazing experiences. We trained very hard, and we were super fit. We used to train with a player called Ian Peter-Budge. It was usually just the three of us. Ian would come and stay at our place for a few days, and at other times we would go to his home. He lived about an hour away and had a tennis court in his backyard too. There were other very promising young players who joined us from time to time such as Ottavio Boron, Antony Hearnden and Kieran Carroll (who, curiously enough, is my stepbrother now, but that's another story). I remember my best mate at the time, Andrew Fox, would ride his bike beside me as I ran alongside. Ian, Q and I would run on the beach where there were large black rocks and boulders; we would aim to touch each one as we ran as fast as we could, trying to build up rapid foot speed. Q was never the quickest, but he had the best endurance and perseverance, and a never-say-die attitude.

I remember once a few years later that he ran a full marathon of 42 kilometres with tennis shoes on and no training at all… incredible! We took up boxing at one point because we heard that training for boxing was one of the best ways to get fit and strong, so we joined a boxing gym in Sandringham, bought our own boxing gear, and would regularly spar with each other. We had core workout contests as well as doing upper body strength work and daily court sprints. As for training on the court, we typically spent about 5-6 hours per day practising. This was usually a mixture of technical training, particularly serving, and loads of drills that involved hitting heaps of balls, and lots of running. Of course, we were very competitive and so always finished with playing a set, a tiebreaker or a series of points.

Q was always a little bit quirky, but usually in a good and funny way. He liked being called Q, and one day he asked me if I could shave the letter 'Q' on the back of his head, so I did. He liked it, so each week I would trim his hair and keep the letter Q there. At the time this was very unusual. Most of our mates had mullets - as some of my mates referred to them: "business at the front and party at the back".

Q had a fascination with feathers, and sometimes collected them. This was the era of headbands, and Pat Cash had his own unique, personalised headband. Q wanted his own too, and he asked Mum to make us both headbands with feathers sticking up like the Native Americans (or as we called them at the time American Indians). We didn't usually play doubles together, however on one occasion we decided to, in a tournament in northern New South Wales, and somehow Q was able to convince me to join him in one of his little schemes. We both put the feather headbands on and walked onto the tennis court. There weren't many people watching that day, but we certainly got noticed. I was trying not to laugh. I had a big grin on my face and thought it was hilarious, but Q told me to stop laughing as he wanted it to look as if this was normal. Our opponents looked at us both with strange expressions that basically said, "what the fuck?" We didn't have an umpire for that match, but the referee came out and told us we could wear them for the hit up but had to take them off for the match, which we did. We ended up losing that match, although we had a lot of fun. I think I was too distracted to concentrate and play well, but for Q it was normal and fine. This feathers episode became somewhat infamous - only recently I met someone we used to play tennis with back then whom I had not seen for over 30 years, and he still recalled the feathers with a smile.

Another story that is strong in my memory was a tournament in Sawtell - northern New South Wales again. We stayed in a small three-bedroom house for a week. I organised it all, and Q and I were joined by Ian Peter-Budge and Kieran Carroll. Q was 16, Ian and Kieran 17, and I was the mature one at 18 years of age. Our focus on training, tennis, and good times had precluded us from acquiring anything but rudimentary domestic skills, so after a week we left the place filthy, and a towering pile of unwashed dishes. We used to get up very early in the morning to begin training and run along the perfect white sandy beaches with our shirts off and the wind blowing in our hair. We felt free as we ran along the water's edge, and that wonderful memory will stay with me forever.

The tennis courts were made of loam, a light yellow, grainy surface that was like En-Tout-Cas in Melbourne or a faster version of the European clay. Q was just starting to really hit his straps and playing incredibly well for a 16-year-old competing against older and more experienced players. He loved the slower surfaces, winning his first round in the qualifying event, and was playing one of the top seeds for a place in the last round before the main draw. Getting into the main draw would have given him a world ranking and a ticket to entry into other tournaments. He won the first set against his older, more experienced and highly ranked opponent. I was so proud of my little brother. I thought then that he truly was going to make it as a professional tennis player. At that point, he was better than me and I knew it. All his hard work and dedication were beginning to pay off. He was lean, fit, strong, and single-minded, but he was still very young and vulnerable.

He was winning in the second set as well, and looked like he would go on to win the match. At the change of ends late in the second set, his opponent said something to him. I'm not quite sure what it was - something like "If you beat me, I'm going to knock your block off." Q crumbled and didn't win another game. This was the sad reality of professional tennis, even at the lower levels of the Satellite Circuit. Q had never encountered this in junior tennis, nevertheless it was rife at the Open level. He took a little while to recover from this, and he wrote a letter to Mum in his scrawling script about the match:

> "I was up 5-1, then Blight called me an arsehole, threatened to punch me out, and said I was the worst player in the tournament, so my temperament couldn't take it. Shots wise I am sure I could be a great clay court player, but I need to improve my temperament drastically. I try to, but on the tennis court my soul departs my body. I have practically no control over my actions."

I didn't know at the time that this was what the other player had said until Q told me later. I wish I had known. I certainly would have said something, although I'm not sure it would have made much difference.

Craig – my life is difficult too

Before my older brother Craig was born, Mum had two stillbirths at around six months. Both were intensely painful for Mum and Dad, who only found out after Craig's birth what the problem was: she had an incompetent cervix, which meant that as soon as the baby got too big or heavy, she would go into premature labour because the cervix would open, and she only needed a small stitch to prevent this from happening again. Mum went into hospital very early - about three months into her pregnancy with Craig - to ensure she was monitored and didn't do anything to put her third pregnancy at risk. She was never allowed out of bed, so she was bored and taught herself to knit to pass the time. Craig arrived six weeks prematurely, but alive and well. He was physically very strong, and, unlike many premature babies, he didn't lose weight. Mum and Dad were relieved, but to this day we are not sure about this next detail - however it is a reasonable assumption that Craig may have lacked oxygen when he was born. Mum has repeatedly wondered about this, although she can't recall exactly what the doctors said. Her paediatrician was called Dr White and, when Craig was only a few months old, Dr White said "this child will be behind until he is about five or six years old." This was such a blunt message, but it proved true far beyond that. Despite this, Mum was mightily relieved and happy that her third attempt at having a child was successful, and she seemed to have a happy, healthy, strong little boy.

Although I've mentioned Craig's athletic ability, he always struggled academically and socially. He attended Narre Warren North Primary School until the end of Year 6, and then he moved to Haileybury College in Year 7 (or what was then called Form 1). It was a very high-achieving school academically, and Craig only lasted for a little over 12 months as it was too hard for him. His cognitive capacity was much lower than normal, and although he was not diagnosed with any illness at that point, intellectually he was slow. He was later tested, and he had an IQ of 70, which showed a mild intellectual disability.

After Haileybury, Craig moved to Tenaden in Belgrave Heights. It was a small independent school that only operated from 1971 to 1980, the opposite to Haileybury College, and catered to kids who didn't fit into mainstream schools. But for Craig it was too far in the other direction and didn't give him the structured environment he needed, and he lasted just two terms. Craig reflects that "Haileybury was too rigid and Tenaden was too slack." In 1978, he moved to Endeavour Hills Technical School, where he survived for a year, successfully completing Year 9. My parents thought this might be the end of his schooling, and he got a job working as a service station attendant in Dingley, but in the middle of 1979, it was decided that he would give school another go. Unbeknown to Mum, Dad had spoken to Kate and John, good friends of theirs, and asked if Craig could live with them for a year and attend Broadmeadows High School, and they said had yes. Dad had not consulted Mum or Craig, but somehow, they both agreed to this, and Craig went to Broadmeadows High where he successfully completed Year 10.

Mum and Dad clearly struggled to know what to do with Craig. They had moved him from school to school with little success, and even out of our home to try their luck with Kate and John, who essentially became his foster parents. They were wonderful people with such patience, compassion, kindness, and generosity. To this day, Craig has incredibly fond memories and a deep affection for them both, particularly Kate, who had a very nurturing approach. After that year, Craig returned home and went to Highett High School - his sixth school, and the fifth in five years. He tried his best in Year 11, but it was too much for him academically and he didn't sit the exam or complete the year.

In addition to his academic problems, Craig struggled to fit in socially. He was teased by other boys, and not intellectually smart enough to respond with a wisecrack. The only thing he excelled in and could win at was fighting. He became aggressive and would beat up people who teased him. At home, this was his reaction too, and he often hit Q and me. He hit hard too. I remember one time when he was about 18 and I was 15, he punched me in the middle of my forehead - not a brother's love tap, but a punch that a boxing coach would be proud of. The brutal force of that knock-out blow sent me flying backwards legs in the air, and I crashed to the ground, unconscious. When I came to, I had a solid lump on my forehead - or as we called it a huge eggy. Q and I were so used being belted by Craig that we plotted to get even. At an opportune moment we summoned all our combined strength and without obvious provocation we attacked Craig, winning the battle, although I suspect we paid a dear price for it later.

Occasionally Craig's strength was helpful though. Despite him hitting me regularly, he was very protective too. We were up at Mt Buller for a few days of skiing, and Craig and I were at a pub called the Arlberg Hotel. When I was about 16 or 17, I occasionally had a cigarette. Back in those days, it was considered cool to carry your smokes tucked up under your t-shirt on your shoulder. I walked past a very tall, tough-looking guy, who took one look at me and said "Hey mate, take those smokes off your shoulder." Intimidated, I immediately did, but Craig happened to be nearby and saw us. He immediately came up to me and said "Don't listen to him, put them back up." In a strange kind of comedic act I did as he said, but Craig didn't stop there. He grabbed the beer the other guy was drinking, threw it in his face, and then proceeded to knock him out with one punch. Then we both fled.

Mum and Dad tried lots of things with Craig, but they really didn't know how to cope. On reflection, they were completely unprepared for the challenge of a child with an intellectual impairment. Dad would call Craig lazy, leaving him feeling rejected and unloved. He didn't understand Craig's lack of intellectual capability, and Craig thought I was the golden child whereas he was the unloved one. When Craig was between 14 and 17, Dad and he would have very physically aggressive fights, and by the time Craig was about 17, he was too strong for Dad to handle. Once Dad got so upset and angry that he threw hot coffee in Craig's face. Mum sometimes ended up slapping him because she was so frustrated that she didn't know what else to do. He was 17 when Mum and Dad asked him to leave home and fend for himself. Yet he was still only a child as his intellectual age was much less than that. He moved out and survived, but not well.

Unfortunately, despite their best efforts, Mum's and Dad's behaviour towards Craig, and their combined parenting approach, were the exact opposite to what Craig yearned for. He needed love, compassion, kindness, and understanding. Mum did her best most of the time, however sometimes her frustration got in the way. Dad just didn't know how to show those qualities. He was an intellectual genius, but as with many people who are highly intelligent cognitively, he had very low emotional intelligence and it showed in his inability to give Craig the emotional support he craved. Craig was always likely to struggle because of his intellectual disability, but his own emotional problems could have been reduced with more compassion and understanding. His anger throughout his teenage years and early adulthood could have been managed better, and he was frequently frustrated because he couldn't do things other people could do. Craig was desperate for love and approval from Dad, but never got it. To this day, his sense of his own value and worth is extremely low. He doesn't believe in himself, and he doesn't think he is worthy of love, which has had a negative effect on his self-confidence and self-respect, showing up in many aspects of his life, particularly in his relationships with women, where he allows them to be disrespectful of him and yet continues to forgive them and not hold them accountable. His low self-esteem and self-belief prevent him from finding the courage to establish boundaries around what is acceptable behaviour.

It feels like I'm criticising Mum and Dad unfairly for poor parenting, and in a way, I am, although I'm not saying it was intentional. I think about how my father was raised in the 1940s and '50s. Times were different back then. People said children should be seen and not heard, and mothers would say things like "wait until your father comes home." The insinuation was that your father wouldn't be as understanding as your mother. He was supposed to be the disciplinarian and not the empathic one, although mothers in those days could also dish out punishment. Mum used to say "I'll wash your mouth out with soap" when we accidentally let slip a dirty or naughty word. These views were common back then, and parents tended not to be as understanding as they are today. Some people believe that we have gone too far the other way now and are not strict enough with this generation of children.

It is impossible to say what is right or wrong in terms of parenting styles. No doubt a balance of compassion and support combined with clear boundaries is the aim today, however exactly what that balance looks like is unclear. Dad was raised by his parents to be well educated so that he could make a good living. He focused solely on being 'the provider', typical of his generation. Men were not usually expected to show a lot of empathy as well as being the provider and disciplinarian. Our father was doing what he thought was best, even though, with hindsight 50 years later, it appears that this wasn't what Craig wanted or needed.

Despite Craig's considerable difficulties, he has done remarkably well. He trained with the St Kilda Football Club Under 19s team for some time and played a few games with them, but unfortunately was not able to make the team permanently. I suspect this had very little to do with his physical capabilities and all to do with his cognitive deficits. Craig started an apprenticeship in Painting and Decorating at the age of 18, but it only lasted ten months. He was a thorough and meticulous painter and did a great job, however he was slow. I recall a time about ten years later when Craig painted a bedroom in my home. He did a perfect job, but instead of taking about two days, it took him seven, working from early morning to late in the day. He tried a second apprenticeship under another qualified painter, but it only lasted two months, and then he got a job in a factory for a little over six months, but he hated it and struggled daily. One job he did like was as a gardener for Sandringham Council. He had been out of work for a while and the government, through the Commonwealth Employment Services (CES), helped him find the job. He enjoyed the green parks, mowing lawns, and generally being outdoors doing something physical and in nature. Unfortunately, this was only a contract position, and the contract ran its course, and he was out of a job again. One of his last jobs was as a taxi driver. Craig loved driving taxis. He was a decent driver and enjoyed talking to people. In a way this was an ideal job for him and lasted a few years until they upgraded some of the technology relating to the system of responding to a call to pick up the next client. This was too complicated for him, and the end of his taxi-driving days.

Craig's last attempt at holding down a permanent job involved car detailing. In 2006, he got a job for Scott Morgan Cars. He enjoyed that and stayed for nine months. It was mundane work, but Craig felt useful, and it was something he did well. Friday was the busiest day - he washed, cleaned, and detailed 60-70 cars every Friday, and worked late into the evening having started early in the morning. Beyond the car detailing work, he also helped with a variety of daily chores including putting the car dealership flags out in front of the property in the morning to

Craig - after he finished the Big M Melbourne Marathon

show potential customers that they were open for business, picking up rubbish from the bins, vacuuming the office, and cleaning the toilets. The culture at Scott Morgan Cars was supportive, and Craig felt accepted and valued. Unfortunately, there was a water shortage in Victoria due to a drought across the state, which meant they were not able to wash as many cars because water was rationed. Craig had been the last cleaner to join the company, therefore he was the first to be laid off. This was extremely discouraging, because it was a steady job that gave him a sense of accomplishment.

Nonetheless, he was able to use this experience to successfully apply for a similar role in Frankston, but while the actual work was the same, the company culture was not so positive. It was an unprofessional environment where the team members, including the manager, bullied, upset, and belittled Craig, and generally made his days miserable. Once six to eight of them lined up like the Blues Brothers with sunglasses on and stared at Craig while he washed a car. They thought it was funny, but Craig felt humiliated, and very upset. He felt low and emotionally abused and questioned the type of people in this world and their level of humanity. As a result, he lost trust in people and left after only two months, and then he did not want to go back to work anywhere.

Perhaps his greatest success at this time was deciding to run a marathon. As a teenager, Craig had started drinking a lot of alcohol as a way of fitting in socially and to cope with life's challenges. However, he was smart enough to realise that alcohol was not good for him and so he gave it up in his early twenties and has never had a drink since. He took up running instead, and ran in the Big M Melbourne Marathon in 1984, finishing very respectably. Craig had a little trouble with eczema, particularly on his hands where he would get painful cracks in his fingers, and I have a poignant image of him running for hours wearing a pair of white gloves to protect his hands and fingers from bleeding. I was so proud of Craig for running the marathon. It showed that despite all his difficulties, he had remarkable persistence and determination, which I think gave him confidence in his achievements.

Reflections on historical changes in parenting

Freud once listed bringing up children as one the three "impossible professions". I don't agree that it is an impossible profession, but I do think it is one of the most challenging aspects of life - although also the most rewarding at times. As new theoretical insights in psychological and social science have emerged, and as dramatic social changes have affected our family lives, there has been an increasing level of social intervention designed to support parents in rearing children. Our beliefs on appropriate parenting are influenced by our own childhood experiences and our knowledge and understanding of the psychology of childhood development. This topic has seen a burgeoning of research in psychology and education over the last 40 years.

Views on child development have evolved over many decades. Way back in 1698, the British philosopher John Locke considered that a child came into the world as a tabula rasa or clean slate, and the child's experiences determined what would be written on the slate. Late in 1953, the behaviourist Skinner saw children's development as an outcome of rewards and punishments in which parents occupy a central place, but since then it has been recognised that nature and nurture are inextricably linked. In 1979, Bronfenbrenner presented compelling arguments that the contribution of the environment includes the fact that the family is affected by the norms of its community and society. Perhaps the most significant historical events in parenting in Australia have been the emergence of the women's movement, the availability of the contraceptive pill and better education for women, and the subsequent changes in their social roles. These changes began in the 1960s and led to the passing of the Equal Opportunity Act in 1977 in Victoria and South Australia, so that there was a rapid increase in the number of women in the workforce. This led in turn to an increasing reliance on non-familial childcare.

Around this time the nature of support given by governments changed. Interventions in many aspects of life were reduced, creating a gap in availability of services to help disadvantaged families to adjust to complex and difficult circumstances. Understanding the historical issues relating to families and these different dynamics helps us make sense of changing views and advice on the most appropriate parenting. In 1967, Baumrind showed that the combination of warmth and authoritative parenting resulted in optimal child outcomes, whereas cold and punitive approaches or the laissez-faire approach of the permissive parent were more likely to lead to poorer child adjustment. Thereafter, parenting advice focused on firm but warm control.

Historically, most literature on parenting was about the role of the mother. The fathers received far less attention but, as the women's movement grew, there was more concentration on fathering, and in the 1960s and '70s cultural norms began changing. Men were able to participate in social processes connected with pregnancy and birth, which helped some begin to explore and develop their nurturing capacities. Fathers increasingly became recognised as competent caregivers.

As I reviewed the research and literature on parenting over the years, I reflected on my own experiences of our cultural norms and societal expectations. Australian society has undergone enormous changes since the 1970s and '80s. The way parents raise children is dramatically different. Parents didn't micro-manage our time as children. We did have swimming and tennis lessons after school, and they were fun, but they were less planned and scheduled than today. We became self-reliant and independent earlier and had a lot more freedom than children today. Parents had less pressure to be perfect. Disciplining children was different. It was not uncommon for parents to spank their children or threaten to 'get the paddle out.'

Play dates weren't even a thing in the '80s. You would simply say to your mother "Mum, I'm going to my friend's house," and she would say OK. You picked your bike up off the front lawn and rode to your friend's house with no helmet on. You dropped your bike on the friend's front lawn, and knocked on the front door and asked your friend's mother if your friend could play. You then hung out with your friend. Simple.

Now the story is a lot different. The child says "Mum, can I have a play date with my friend?" The response is usually "Maybe, let me check my diary. You can see them next Saturday. I'll check with their mum and see if they're free. If not, I'll try the following week." The mums plan for a mutually convenient time and book an appropriate start time for the play date. The visiting child's mum will drive their child to the friend's house with some appropriate snacks. Life has certainly changed, as have our expectations.

The research and our personal experiences of child-rearing have both shown that things are now significantly different. There is a cohesive body of evidence that proves some general principles of positive parenting that are widely accepted, such as warmth, responsivity, consistency, limit-setting, and avoidance of harsh punishment. There is also increasing recognition of children's individuality, and the active role they play in their own development. We also know that the relationship between parent and child is dynamic and bidirectional, therefore parenting practices must fit the child rather than a one-size-fits-all approach. In addition, good parenting in the future will also depend upon whether social environments can support parents raising children, including family support, education, and opportunities for employment, as well as the understanding and appreciation that the responsibility of parents is both challenging and rewarding.

How does all this relate to my brother Craig? Hindsight is a wonderful gift that we humans have, and so it is easy in 2024 to look back at parenting practices in the 1970s and '80s and see the flaws from today's vantage point. However, when you understand the history of parenting trends and the norms of the society of the time, you gain a more nuanced perspective on the complex factors that were at play in raising children. My mother and father were a part of this potent social context and did their absolute best and what they thought was right. Would Craig have had a better life if he had been raised differently? Possibly or probably! I don't have answers, but I do think it is worth pausing and reflecting on these aspects of my story.

Nana – it's in the family

Dad's Mum, Ethel Fricke, my grandmother (Nana as we called her), was a character. I remember her well. She had a big impact on me as a young boy. She was a passionate Collingwood Football Club supporter. Dad followed Fitzroy Football Club, and so as the dutiful son I too followed Dad's team until I was about six. However, I used to stay with Nana and Pa at their home in Northcote, and Nana took me to a Collingwood match. I loved it. She had a cute little koala toy that played the Collingwood theme song when you wound it up. There was an inspirational Collingwood forward called Phil Carman, who kicked ten goals in a match, and it was all over the newspapers. That sealed it - I changed my allegiance from Fitzroy to Collingwood. Nana was delighted. My father didn't say anything.

I didn't know about Nana's mental health issues until many years later. I only assumed that she had some problems in her very last years when she suffered from dementia and exhibited quite odd behaviour but, unbeknownst to me, she had mental health difficulties throughout her life. On one occasion apparently Nana was in a car screaming loudly and needed to be restrained to prevent her harming herself. She had several episodes over the years, but they were never mentioned. There is no doubt in my mind now that she also suffered from severe clinical depression, never professionally diagnosed.

My grandfather Norm (or Pa as I called him) was a kind, gentle, simple man. He was born in 1900, and illegally put his age up to try to fight in World War I, although he failed in his attempt to join the Great War and put it down to do the same in World War II. He was successful this time and supported the war effort by making roads up in Darwin. Apart from that, he worked in a shoe factory for his entire life. He never owned a car and cycled to the factory each day. He rode his bike everywhere. Mum called Norm "Pop", and she called Nana "Muff". Mum would often ask my grandfather "How's Muff, Pop?" and he would say "She's in bed, Jude." It is very sad to look back on this story and these times, only to realise that Nana needed help. While Pa was a kind man, and tried to understand, their only solution seemed to be for Ethel to sleep, so she stayed in her room for days until she somehow got better or felt well enough to resume day-to-day activities.

Back in the 1960s and '70s, mental illness was viewed very differently. Disturbed people were usually confined and separated from the broader society. Mental illness was out of sight, and therefore mostly out of everyone's mind. Whilst Nana did not end up in an asylum, many people were locked up in asylums, which were separated from large population centres. It wasn't until the 1980s or '90s that the idea of deinstitutionalisation took place in Australia. Then there was a move to reduce hospital beds, and to grow community services and provide pharmacological and psychological interventions. It was not until 1987 that the antidepressant medication fluoxetine (Prozac) was introduced, and doctors began to prescribe it to depressed patients. This treatment revolutionised how depression was treated. Prior to this, mental asylums were notorious for their harsh treatments, which included the use of restraints, isolation, electroshock therapy, ice baths, forced drugging, and even lobotomies. Sometimes I feel that we have such a long way to go in the way we take care of people with mental illnesses, however when I look back on this period, I am relieved that we have in fact already come a long way.

Pa died in 1983, and Nana came to live with us. This was very kind of my mother given Nana was not her mother, and she would have to look after Nana because Dad would not help. Nana lived with us for the last couple of years of her life, and I cherish the many fun times we shared as she became frailer. She had an irreverent, naughty side as well as being what we boys called a bit strange. I remember that when I was about five, I went to Sunday School, although we were not a religious family at all. Perhaps it was with Nana, who was doing just enough to keep on the right side of the Lord should she need him. I wore a red jumpsuit of some description, had blond hair, and was obviously a little bit cute. The person up front leading the Sunday School session looked at me and asked, "Would that little girl in red please come up to the front with me?" I was extremely embarrassed when I realised that he was talking to me and exclaimed "I'm not a girl! I'm a boy!" Nana loved the story, and for the rest of her life she would tell it to tease me. She would say in a funny girlish voice "Would that little girl in red…"

In 1985, when I was in the US, we had to be creative about the way we stayed in touch with each other. Mum used a cassette tape to record family dinner conversations over several nights and would send it to me when it was full. I would listen to the tape many times, and then make my own recording and send it back to Mum and the family. I recall Nana's voice saying "Hayden, it's your old granny here…" and she would go on to say something funny. Now I think how similar some of her qualities were to Q's humour and mischievousness. I don't think we used the word 'dementia' back then, but in the last year or so of her life she became stranger and was clearly suffering from some form of dementia. In those later years, she was taking medication, but I'm not sure exactly what it was - probably an antidepressant, something like temazepam. Nana, like most patients, was not always good about taking her medication. It affected her strangely - she used to gyrate her hips in a slightly sexy way, which was a bit weird. In general terms, dementia is a loss of memory, language, problem-solving, and other thinking capacities, severe enough to interfere with daily life. Alzheimer's disease is the most common cause of dementia, contributing to 60-70 percent of cases. Nana believed that Norm was outside calling for her, and Yvette frequently found her late at night looking intently out of the second-storey window and tapping on it. She would explain to Yvette that Norm was out there, and Yvette would say "Pa died two years ago" to which Nana responded "Yes, I know that, but he's out there waiting for me."

On New Years' Eve in 1985, while I was in the US and Mum, Dad and Yvette were on holiday at Bateman's Bay in New South Wales, Q stayed at home with Nana. A lovely lady, Julie, who had looked after us kids on and off over the years, was staying there too, mainly to look after Nana whose mind had almost gone, and she had lost the ability to function and take care of herself. At about two or three in the morning, Nana climbed out of her second-floor bedroom window, trying to reach Norm. She fell to the ground and spent the rest of what must have been an agonising night in terrible pain, no doubt lapsing in and out of consciousness. Early the next morning, our next-door neighbours discovered her, clutching to life and uttering barely audible moans as she lay in a pool of blood with a broken pelvis. They alerted Q and Julie, who came out to the horrible scene, and stayed with Nana until the ambulance arrived. She lived long enough to be transported to hospital, and Q and Craig went with her to offer what love and support they could. Julie called Mum and Dad, who immediately started driving home, but Nana had other plans, and she died the day before they arrived. She seemed in a hurry to be with Norm, and she was finally at peace.

It was a terrible and traumatic way to end her life. I was not aware of it at the time, but a 2019 study by Ji Hyun An et al. found that among people with cognitive impairment caused by dementia, the risk of accidental death increases significantly. There are 47 million people with dementia worldwide, and this number is expected to rise to 131 million by 2050. It is unbearable to know that accidental death - particularly in a traffic accident - is more likely and yet usually preventable. Overall, dementia is the seventh leading cause of death. It is a terrible illness, and the circumstances around Nana's death were as shocking and upsetting as you can imagine.

It is hard to say how much this affected Q, however it certainly caused him considerable stress and anxiety. When you combine this disturbing and traumatic episode with his own mental challenges and his difficulty in communicating and talking through things in a reasonably rational and normal manner, I feel that it had a significant impact.

My father also had a sister, my Aunty Joan. She was nine years older than Dad, and we didn't have a lot to do with her. She was never really spoken about, however we now know that she suffered from acute depression, and was often in a psychiatric institution called Mont Park Asylum. Nana and Pa were stoic about it. People were 'committed' to an asylum just like criminals were sent to prison. This was a hospital for mentally ill people and 'the insane'. Patients were routinely restrained with straitjackets, skull caps, and locked boots, and kept in padded cells or confined to small and overcrowded wards and given ECT and other treatments to cure or manage them. Nana and Pa went to visit Joan occasionally, but they never talked about her, even to Mum and Dad. Shortly after both her children, my cousins Garry and Janette, were born, Joan tried to commit suicide twice by cutting her wrists. Neither attempt was successful, and Nana and Pa looked after Garry and Janette while she recovered.

I'm relieved that we don't treat people like this anymore. That is, we don't lock them away in asylums where they treat them with dreadful equipment like skull caps. However, we still fail to speak openly about mental illness, and people still experience a range of uncomfortable emotions when confronted by it. They may be scared, unsure, embarrassed, guilty, frustrated or angry - all normal human emotions but frequently ignored because they are too hard to deal with, so we act as if nothing were wrong.

Why is it hard to talk about mental illness?

Although a growing proportion of our population suffers from mental health issues, it is still a subject that creates a high level of discomfort. Why do people hesitate to talk about something so prevalent? One of the key reasons is stigma, where we tend to have a negative attitude towards a person because of certain habits or characteristics. Stigma may adversely influence how others see someone so that they treat them differently, which may lead to a sense of shame, fear or loneliness. Shame and isolation contribute to poor mental health, and one of our greatest needs as humans is to feel that we belong. Since we want to be loved and approved of, letting people know that we have psychological problems may lead to a sense of loneliness and a lack of belonging.

Mental health stigma can also create a vicious cycle of self-criticism, which forces many people to endure their emotional impairments silently, and these feelings are exacerbated by unrealistic cultural expectations, stereotypical beliefs, and toxic masculinity - external influences that can lead to trauma and harsh discrimination.

Mental illness can be particularly challenging for some racial and ethnic communities. In Australia, we are a multicultural society with many different nationalities living together, and this may be a major barrier to effective conversations. For example, in some Asian cultures seeking professional help for mental illness is seen as weakness and against the cultural values of a healthy family. This leads to strong feelings of shame, so to avoid the shame people stay silent.

A lack of understanding can lead to fear and stigma too, and I have repeatedly seen inaccurate or misleading media representations of mental illness. A study in 2020 looked at the popular film *Joker* (2019), where the lead character is a person with mental illness who becomes extremely violent. The study found that viewing the film "was associated with higher levels of prejudice toward those with mental illness."

Unfortunately, this stigma is universal. A 2016 study demonstrated that there is no country, society, or culture where people with mental illness have the same societal value as people without a mental illness.

Beyond stigma, many friendship groups only encourage fun and positivity and fail to allow space for vulnerability. Being vulnerable means risking getting hurt, and people often fear that if others know our insecurities or secrets, they may be rejected. Vulnerability may also mean revealing our weaknesses and giving up control. We may feel that we will be judged for admitting to our deepest fears and worries. When we are rejected, it hurts us emotionally. Our brains process this type of pain similarly to physical pain, and the cost of vulnerability is a potential ache and discomfort we usually try to avoid.

Brené Brown, well known for her research into vulnerability, suggests we learn to be more vulnerable, and that vulnerability is not weakness at all, but shows strength and courage. She demonstrates through her work that it is a significant and essential component of building healthy, kind, and compassionate relationships. To overcome our fears of rejection and isolation, we need to accept and love ourselves first, and then we can be authentic as we build our self-esteem and confidence. This is the aim, but the journey is difficult and requires great courage.

Another barrier to talking about mental health is the fear of being judged. People with low self-esteem are more sensitive to this as they already have a negative view of themselves, which exacerbates the emotional pain. There are a many emotional responses to people trying to open up and talk about their mental health issues, and some may feel humiliated, exposed and foolish. Many people feel embarrassed, self-conscious, and uncomfortable about how they think others perceive them.

Also, people sometimes fear revealing their mental health challenges, and burdening and overwhelming those they tell. It is not fun to be with someone who is negative, so we want to hang out with positive, optimistic, upbeat people, whereas frequently people with mental health concerns are perceived to be weak or even hysterical. If someone says they are feeling anxious, they are often told not to worry or that everything will be OK. Sadly, this response leads to their feelings being dismissed, and to their not having a safe space to share their thoughts and emotions. Minimising people's feelings does more harm than good.

Across our society, we have different benchmarks and expectations about what it means to be functional, and what is acceptable for others to maintain a relationship with us. Those who fail to live up to what others consider normal may be considered dysfunctional, and excluded from social gatherings, and for many people with mental health issues, the mere thought of attending social events is often exhausting, draining, and overwhelming, which further exacerbates their isolation and loneliness.

Social media has made it harder for us all to be honest, authentic, and vulnerable. In today's world where image is so important, particularly to young people, disclosing mental health issues may harm our image and reputation.

Many people without a mental problem worry that they will say the wrong thing. Talking about these issues can be quite emotionally raw, and everyone has their own boundaries, but recognising them can be complex. We often want to make awkward, uncomfortable or distressing feelings go away, and so we say things to make it all OK - however, we all need to be better at sitting down with the discomfort and just listening.

Family breakdown – divorce and chaos

While Q was going through his nervous breakdown, Craig was struggling to live independently, Yvette was 14 and trying to work out what was happening in her family, and I was in the US attempting to be successful at tennis. Several other significant events were also taking place: Mum and Dad were battling to keep their marriage together - they were a typical couple of their era, with both undertaking their respective traditional family roles well, and we kids didn't really think too much about it... what kids do?

Mum was the homemaker, and very active in the community. She had joined the local Scouts committee, she was a member of the Australian Labour Party, and President of the Labour Women's Involvement Group, and was on the committee of the Doveton Community Health Centre. Mum has always been a regular contributor to the communities that she lived in and has focused on supporting causes that matter to her, which, typically, have involved fighting for the less well-off.

Dad provided for his family tremendously well. He had moved from being brought up in relative poverty to being able to afford most things. When he was a child, he had had to sleep outside on a single bed under the back veranda of their house with only a green shade cloth for protection from the elements, because there was no room inside for him. His parents had a small two-bedroom house, and his elder sister Joan slept in the second bedroom. In winter, when it was bitterly cold

**Family in earlier and happier times
(from left to right – Yvette, Craig, Dad, Mum, Hayden, Q)**

and he only had a couple of thin blankets to keep him warm, he used to pull the covers over his head and read for hours with a torch until he eventually fell asleep. The house did not have a bathroom or running hot water so, to keep clean, once a week they would fill up a big tub with hot water, and then Dad, Joan, and their mum and dad would take turns getting into a warm bath. At one point, Norm and Ethel were so poor that they couldn't afford toilet paper and so they cut the Yellow Pages in the telephone book into little squares and used that. This was Dad's early life. I should point out that, while by today's standards this would be thought of as poverty, back in then it was not extreme poverty. He had a roof over his head, and his parents owned their home. His parents made him feel less well off than was necessary, and were always worried about money, but in fact, after Nana and Pa died and the house was sold, Dad found thousands of dollars in cash all over the house - in curtains, under the beds, and in the shed out the back. In the 1970s and early '80s, Malcolm Fraser, who was Prime Minister from 1975-83, said "put your money under the bed", and Nana and Pa took him seriously. I have also learnt that wiping your bum with the Yellow Pages was not uncommon, particularly in country toilets out the back.

Dad studied hard through primary school, and then attended Northcote High School, doing so well that he was awarded a scholarship to prestigious Melbourne High School when he was 16 for his final year. At the end of Year 12, he was offered two bursaries to help with his law degree at the University of Melbourne, and took the more generous Dafydd Lewis Scholarship, which paid for his books and fees, and provided enough money for him to buy clothes. He also worked as a football umpire, and took various factory jobs to make ends meet.

Having excelled at university, and completed his law degree at 21, Dad did so well that he won a Ford Foundation scholarship to attend the University of Pennsylvania and sit his Master of Laws. After his year in the US, he returned and married Judy, my Mum, in 1959. They had got engaged before Dad left for the US and were married a week after he came home.

Dad became a barrister in 1962, and while he was kept busy in the early days, there was little money coming in because solicitors often did not pay for up to 12 months. However, by the early 1970s his practice at the bar was thriving, and he became a Queens Counsel (QC) in 1979, a considerable achievement and an honour. He worried that the high fees a QC had to charge would mean that solicitors would be reluctant to engage him, and his upbringing meant that he was frequently worried about money and feared not being able to provide despite his success.

Notwithstanding this, Dad adapted well to his new position, as he did all his life. Only four years later, in 1983, he accepted a position as a County Court Judge. This was very prestigious, and an explicit recognition of years of hard work, and his intelligence and capabilities as a barrister and QC.

His success meant that growing up we led a good life. My childhood was wonderful until I was about 19. There was enough money to send us to private schools, although neither Q nor Craig was able to take advantage of this. We lived in Brighton, a beautiful suburb by the beach in Melbourne, in a large home with a tennis court and swimming pool. Mum and Dad didn't desire material possessions, flashy cars or lead an ostentatious life. They were both cautious with money, and never wanted to look too extravagant. Dad was single-minded, and this meant that we didn't spend much time with him. He would leave early in the morning before we got up, and he'd get home just in time for dinner. He usually joined us, but sometimes he ate, accompanied by a bottle of red wine, watching a documentary show called Four Corners or the ABC News by himself, and would then go into his study and work into the night.

Mum was left to do almost all the parenting, and she did it well, showing a very caring, nurturing side and giving us love and affection. She also disciplined us, often chasing us around the house, hitting us with a feather duster - not the feather end! No doubt it was enormously difficult to find time to maintain a quality relationship while Dad focused on building his career and providing for the family, but Mum was totally invested in her children. As Q and Craig began to have more obvious problems as teenagers, there was increasing pressure on a marriage that was already strained. They didn't quite know how to handle Craig, and frequently disagreed about how to deal with Q. Dad was not at all supportive of Q's tennis aspirations, whereas Mum tried to help him. He had nothing else.

About ten years earlier, Mum and Dad had separated for about two weeks. One day Dad just left us all without saying a word. To this day, Mum still doesn't know where he went or why he left. Obviously, she was concerned about what would happen, and wondered why he had left, where he had gone, if he would come back - but as children we didn't even notice. Dad was hardly ever around anyway. It is sad that none of us asked where Dad was. We probably didn't even think about him... I guess. Mum is such a strong, determined, and stoic woman - and despite her worries, she just kept busy taking care of us. She didn't tell anyone then, and only told me recently. Her aim was simply to take care of her children and get on with life. I find this quite remarkable. More surprisingly, when Dad came home, they didn't even discuss it. They simply resumed their marriage without ever talking about it. Mum just knew that Dad was private and secretive and would not want to discuss it.

Over the years we were witness to many arguments, which over time grew in intensity. They were usually at night when we were upstairs. I assume they both thought we could not hear them, but the arguments were very loud and disturbing. They never resulted in physical abuse, but they were painful and heated, although Mum doesn't seem to recall them. Perhaps she has unconsciously blocked them out of her memory, but I certainly remember them, and feel slightly uncomfortable thinking about it now, even though that was 40 years ago.

Eventually this all took a toll. Mum and Dad separated in March 1986, only three months after Q had found Nana barely alive. The separation was immensely emotional and traumatic for everyone. One morning, after increasingly bitter arguments, Dad drove off to work and left a note for Mum. It read "I think it is best for all of us if I leave..." That was typical of Dad. He was unable to talk about his emotions or feelings or to explain things. That note was the best he could do. Yvette, who was in Year 9, came downstairs to get ready for school. Mum told her about the note. Yvette was very upset and continued to cry in the weeks and months that followed and struggled to concentrate at school. Dad didn't call her for a few months, not even to say hello, so she had zero contact with him. He just got up and left. As a father myself of three children, I struggle to comprehend this. And then one day, he rang her out of the blue and asked her to join him for dinner.

Dad did not call or invite Craig or Q to dinner. It was just Yvette. She felt guilty that Dad favoured her and me, leaving Craig and Q out. He was totally unaware of this bias, but Yvette and I had often observed it. However, at the age of 14 or 15 she didn't have the courage to say anything to him. Dad was living in an apartment in the city, and asked her to take a train in, which she did even though she had never done it before. They had dinner together, and then she caught the train home again. This time it was dark and late at night. It's hard to imagine it now, looking back. She had never been on a train to the city by herself, let alone at night. It's hard to understand why Mum or Dad didn't drive her. Dad just didn't think of things like that. Although he had a brilliant mind for the law, he lacked consideration for others.

While this was happening, I was in the US at college. I recall wanting to come back and fix all the problems - my family was falling apart, and I was on the other side of the world. I wanted to come home and find a way to bring my parents back together and help Q to sort his life out. I found myself crying a lot at night and feeling awfully helpless. One night shortly after Mum and Dad separated and I was not coping well emotionally or mentally, a good friend, Steven Angelides, and I bought some alcohol and drove out to a remote area. We sat in the car, played loud music for a few hours and got drunk together. I assume Steven drove us back to college, but I can't remember. When I came home from the US a few months later, Yvette and I were able to support each other, and together we courageously insisted Dad ask Q and Craig when he invited us to dinner. Looking back now, it's amazing to think that we had

Family breakdown – divorce and chaos

to do that when we were only 15 and 19. Again, Dad had no idea how it would have felt to Craig and Q. It was a massive blind spot for him.

The emotional side of our parents' separation was raw and intense. I was shocked to observe how love can turn into hatred. I remember a scene about eight years after their separation, when Lynne and I had our engagement party at Yvette's home. Of course, we had to invite both Mum and Dad, but since anger, contempt, and frustration were still high we did our best to keep them apart. Unfortunately, that didn't last long, and at one point Mum became so irate that she threw a glass of red wine in Dad's face. A year later at our wedding, we spent quite a bit of time organising the seating arrangements to ensure they were at opposite ends of the venue.

Divorce and the Impact on Children

Sadly, over 30 percent of first marriages in Australia end in divorce, and so do up to 60 percent of second marriages. Perhaps people who get married a second time have not learnt much. The average length of a marriage in Australia is 12 years, with separation before divorce occurring on average after eight years. My parents divorced after 27 years, so I guess that's a win! Most people marry at 25-29 and get divorced at 40-49. Mum was 49 and Dad was 51 when they separated, so in this regard they were slightly older than average. Research shows that relationships require a lot of time and effort. While you may fall in love in your mid-twenties, this is not enough to sustain a long-term relationship. Research also shows that marriages tend to end primarily due to inattention and not nurturing the relationship. Many divorced couples report communication problems, loss of connection, or issues of trust, and these were certainly evident in my mother and father's relationship.

Although the average age of children whose parents get divorced is six to seven, frequently it is when the children are teenagers, and the parents have had problems to deal with and are no longer the young couple that was in love several years before. Coping with a family breakdown, separation, and divorce is particularly difficult. All circumstances are unique, and how they impact the family is different. A family grows, develops, and evolves over time. Children are regularly the most affected by a separation, and the breakup of the parental unit brings many changes, physical such as one parent moving to a different home, as well as emotional - all related to the confusion and frustration of not understanding what is happening or why.

Children sometimes protest this situation in unusual ways such as poor academic performance, withdrawal from friends and family, or other problematic behaviours, because they are grieving for the loss of the family unit they have known for their entire life. This grief causes a variety of emotions, including anxiety, depression, helplessness, misery, guilt, numbness, anger, and confusion. Some children may have trouble with emotional attachment and suffer from lack of self-esteem caused by a fear of abandonment and of not being good enough to be loved. Often, they are not conscious of these fears.

The factors that have the greatest impact on children include the degree and duration of hostile conflict, the quality of parenting provided over time, and the parent-child relationship. Children are good at sensing hostility between parents. In our case, we were very aware that Mum nursed anger and resentment towards Dad. To his credit, Dad never said anything negative about Mum, but she certainly shared her bitterness with us. She did not realise that this was very unhelpful, though to be fair she probably had more things to be frustrated with, but we didn't need to hear them. As with many family separations, we struggled with balancing divided loyalties between Mum and Dad. Mum had always been the one who cared for and supported us, and Dad was seldom around, so it was natural to feel closer to Mum, but we also wanted a relationship with our father. Children in these circumstances often feel disloyal if they still love both parents, and yet one of the parents is openly criticising the other. For us, the open conflict was certainly an ongoing emotional challenge.

It is impossible to say how much Mum and Dad's separation and subsequent divorce troubled each of us. We all had sharp reactions, but I think Yvette and Q were hit the hardest, Yvette because of her age and the fact she was the only one living at home. She was only 14 years old when they separated, and their divorce was finalised on her 16th birthday. Craig had moved out, I was in the US, and Q was travelling too. Q had just turned 17, and it happened at a time when he most needed the support of his parents. He was trying to become a professional tennis player and had the poorest communication and coping skills.

Dad – alcoholism and bipolar disorder

After the shock and the initial intensity of the separation and realisation that this was permanent, we settled into a new life with Mum in the family home. Dad had moved out, and so the positive side was that the arguments stopped. We enjoyed being together. Dinner conversations were fun - lots of banter, silliness, and laughter. However, we rarely saw Dad. He just didn't seem interested in seeing us. He had left and never called. So, we just got on with our lives as a family without a father. In a way, this wasn't a lot different, because he had been an absent father throughout our childhood - yet it was more definitive.

It was not until this separation that I took the time to think about who my father was, the challenges he faced, and the social aspects of his life. Dad had always been socially awkward and uncomfortable. In the early years of the marriage, whenever they went out with friends Dad would have a couple of alcoholic drinks beforehand just so he could relax. He liked to entertain his friends, and often invited barristers, solicitors, and later judges home for a Sunday afternoon of tennis and a barbeque lunch or dinner. Dad loved red wine, and he always had a full glass in his hand. I never thought much about it at the time, but later, I remembered that he drank red wine every night with dinner, usually drink an entire bottle by himself. Dad was an undiagnosed alcoholic. He would drink every day. I used to think an alcoholic was someone who got smashed and was not able to function properly. I guess I had an image of a derelict drunk with unkempt hair wandering around the streets looking forlorn. However,

Dad was mostly able to function well. He had been a highly successful barrister, then QC, then judge. His alcoholism was hidden. It was and still is considered normal to have a drink on social occasions. It was and still is even reasonably normal to have a glass of wine at lunchtime. Dad did that and seemed to function fine. It was just that he didn't stop. He didn't take a day off... ever. It's like he just kept topping up. Sometimes he would get really drunk and act like most drunks do, slurring his words and swaying from side to side, but most of the time it was hard to tell if Dad was drunk or even affected by the alcohol.

There are different types of alcoholics. Alcoholism is the common name for a medical disorder where someone cannot stop drinking alcohol, even when it begins to cause problems. The different forms of alcoholism are characterised by a combination of factors such as the severity of the condition, the behaviours associated with it, and the drinker's demographic profile. I would say that Dad was a functioning alcoholic. Approximately one fifth of the Australian population fits into this category. They are usually middle-aged, educated, stable people, who can keep up with their day-to-day responsibilities, look successful, and are unlikely to seek help outside of a crisis.

Dad's level of drinking would probably have put him in a category known as middle stage alcoholism. It was not a quick high, but rather a staple of his daily life. He had built up a high tolerance for alcohol, his body had adapted to having it in his system, and he was mentally and physically dependent on it. While I never noticed any, he probably would have had withdrawal symptoms without a certain level of alcohol in his body.

Later, Dad's second wife Toni installed a breathalyser in his car so that he had to blow in it to be able to start the engine. That meant less than a 0.05 percent alcohol content in his blood to be able to drive, so frequently he couldn't drive. Toni also set rules to limit his alcohol intake in his last few years. He was not allowed a drink before 5pm, he had to wait 30 minutes between drinks, and he could only have half a bottle of red wine each evening. It is sad to think that it came to this, but it was necessary. Somehow Dad accepted these rules and restrictions, and at some level he seemed to understand that he needed them and needed someone to impose them.

Dad – in his attire as a Judge in the County Court of Victoria

Although alcohol helped Dad feel less anxious in social situations, it didn't reduce his awkwardness. He regularly misread cues and misunderstood the emotional aspects of various interactions. An example of this was when he invited Yvette and me to lunch when I was about 26. We thought it was a bit unusual, and assumed he wanted to talk to us about something reasonably important, however we had no idea what it was about. As soon as we sat down, with no preamble, Dad said "How would you feel if I were to tell you, hypothetically, that Penny is your sister?" Yvette and I both immediately stammered and came up with the same question "Dad, are you saying that Penny is our sister?"

Dad replied "Yes." Both our mouths dropped to the floor. We had a million questions like: "What do you mean?" "How did this happen?" "Who is her mother?" "How long have you known?" "Why didn't you tell us until now?"

Over lunch, Dad told us most of the story, and much more came out over the following months. Penny and Vladimir Antonov had been good friends of the family for about ten years. Penny was ten years older than me, and I first met her when I was about 15. I assumed they were just slightly younger friends of Mum and Dad's. We all liked Penny and got to know her well, but just as friends, so it was a complete shock when Dad told us she was our sister.

It turned out that Dad had had a relationship with a woman called Elaine back at university, prior to meeting Mum, and Elaine fell pregnant with Penny. Dad knew about Elaine's pregnancy, but she was also dating another man, Alan, and initially Dad, assumed that Penny was Alan's daughter. Elaine left university and married Alan. At some point before Dad met Mum, he found out that Penny was his daughter. I'm not sure exactly how much he knew about Penny as she grew up, however he clearly understood that she was his child as the following story demonstrates:

Penny had studied law and got in touch with Dad when he was a judge in the County Court. She made an appointment to see him to discuss something in relation to the law. Dad assumed that she had found out he was her father, and, with his usual awkwardness and lack of emotional intelligence, he blurted out "I suppose you know?" Penny asked, "Know what?" Dad replied, "That I'm your father." Penny had had no idea, and went home and asked her mother, who initially denied it, but eventually a secret that had been carefully kept for over 25 years came out into the open, and we had a half-sister whom we had not grown up with. Over the next 20 years, we all got to know and love Penny and her family. Sadly, she passed away from cancer in 2012.

What I didn't understand until much later was that dad had bipolar disorder. As children we had no concept of this, and like his alcoholism it was never discussed. The stigma of mental illness was terrible, and of course was already in our family. His reputation as a Queen's Counsel and a judge was very important to him, and it would have damaged his standing and image.

Mum recently told me that early on in their relationship Dad decided to see a psychiatrist. He did this by himself without talking to her and was very secretive about it. The psychiatrist put Dad on medication to help with his anxiety. I'm not certain what the medication was, but I think it was probably something like Xanax, which treats anxiety and panic disorders. Dad's anxiety was like a panic disorder in social situations, and he was on medication for many years although he never spoke to Mum or anyone else about it. The only time Mum was involved with Dad's mental health issues was shortly after he saw the psychiatrist. Dad asked Mum if she would talk to him, and she had a session with him without Dad. The psychiatrist told Mum that Dad had said she was very good with him and very patient. They never discussed it again.

I look back on this and realise how far our society has come since then. The stigma surrounding mental health issues was real. Dad would have been judged harshly had they come out in the open, and it would have affected his career. Not talking about mental health issues was the way most people dealt with them and with anxiety, but while it may have been good for his career, it certainly was not helpful for Dad personally. Hiding the problem from everyone meant that it was not managed, and it got worse over the years and led to a secondary illness – alcoholism. Sadly, this still happens today.

People of Mum and Dad's era were usually more secretive about mental health and other personal issues, but Dad's behaviour was often more extreme than other men of his time. Image and reputation were crucial for him, especially since he had risen from poverty and wanted to fit in with a high socio-economic society. Dad's father Norm went bald from alopecia in his early twenties, and Dad was secretly concerned about this. He began losing his hair in his early thirties. One day he came home early from work. This was very unusual. Mum was home. Dad had something covering his head. He didn't say anything to Mum. He walked straight past her and through to the bedroom and stayed there. He had had a hair transplant, but he never said a word to Mum about it.

Bipolar disorder has extreme mood swings that include emotional highs (mania) and lows (depression). Each period can last from days to weeks. During periods of mania, the person is usually abnormally energetic, happy, or irritable. They make impulsive decisions with little regard for the consequences, and there is a reduced need for sleep. Conversely, during periods of depression the individual may have a very negative outlook on life, and the risk of suicide is high with approximately 6% of those suffering from bipolar disorder committing suicide and up to 40% engaging in self-harm.

As far as I know, Dad never tried to harm himself or take his life, but he did impulsive things without any apparent thought or bregard for others. He also bought properties that he believed would be great for some unknown reason, but no thought, planning or discussion went into them. A key criterion for Dad was that the property be cheap. One day he told me that he wanted to buy a holiday house on Phillip Island that the family could all go to together. This was when we were in our twenties, and it was his way of having time with his family again – a noble objective, but he wanted to buy something immediately without forethought, totally on impulse. I didn't realise it at the time, but it was during one of his manic phases. Knowing Dad's history of buying properties, I realised that if I didn't get involved straight away - that very day - we would end up with a tumble-down dump in the middle of nowhere that nobody would want to go to, which would totally defeat the purpose. I got involved. Dad had a very low budget in mind, so we were restricted in what we could buy. Eventually he bought a house in a lovely part of Phillip Island called Ventnor. He put it in the names of his children, and so we each owned a small share. It was about 300 metres from the beach, and although it only had two bedrooms there was a large backyard so people could sleep in tents. I had a young and growing family at the time, and we used the house frequently and loved it. Dad's dream to bring us together didn't happen though - we ended up going down to the island separately as the house was too small for all of us to use at the same time.

I recall vividly that, during one of Dad's manic episodes, he drove to Ventnor. He was quite excited when he told me he had painted the entire outside of the house. He had never discussed doing this with us, even though it was technically ours. He just did it. I was scared just thinking about it, and when I went down to have a look my fears were well founded. He had painted the house a terrible canary yellow, which he thought was inspirational. He had also drawn a map of Phillip Island on the back of the house and painted little birds and music notes along the fence line. Dad was not a good painter, so it looked atrocious. This was part of his illness - it was during his manic phases that he did things like this.

On another occasion, Dad decided he was a handyman, although he was not handy at all. He paved the front and the back entertainment area next to our tennis court and swimming pool with red bricks and happened to put all the bricks the wrong way up. You are meant to have the flat side up, but he laid them with the slightly curved and indented side up, which led to water pooling whenever it rained for years to come. This was during another of his manic periods, when he had boundless energy and believed he could do anything, despite previous evidence to the contrary.

Nor did Dad know how to show love or warmth, but I guess that is typical of men of his generation. His father had probably never told him that he loved him - men just didn't do that very often back in the 1930s and '40s when Dad was growing up, although I have spoken to some of my mates whose fathers were able to break this mould and show their love and affection. I remember one time when Dad said "Hayd," (his affectionate nickname for me) "do you want to come with me to get a burger?" This was unusual. I had never done this with Dad before. However, he meant let's go right now. So off we went in the car together to get a burger. I don't know what the mood was or why I did what I did next, but for some reason I was compelled to say, "I love you, Dad." This took enormous courage, because I had never said it before, and Dad had never told me he loved me. I assume I must have really wanted him to say it back to me, and I saw this small window of opportunity alone in the car with him. His response shattered me. He said, "Don't be ridiculous!" I was gobsmacked. I didn't say anything after that. We drove on in silence, bought our burgers, ate them, and drove home.

Yvette recently told me about a similar experience. Dad was in hospital when he was in his early seventies with a life-threatening problem. We all rushed there to be with him, and potentially to say our goodbyes. Yvette had never told Dad that she loved him and, thinking this was likely to be the end of the road for him, she took a deep breath and said, "I love you, Dad." Clearly, she had hoped for the same thing I did... to hear him say it too. But again, he couldn't, and he simply responded with "Yeah." On a more positive note, in the last year of his life he was able to tell Yvette he loved her, although she thinks it was because dementia made him act differently.

Reflecting on my father

I'm not quite sure what factors contributed to Dad's inability to say I love you, or even to show any positive emotion towards his children, but I suspect several elements: alexithymia is when a person has difficulty experiencing, identifying, and expressing emotions. It is not a mental health disorder but does have links with various conditions including autism. Up to 13% of the population in Australia have alexithymia, men almost twice as frequently as women. Alexithymia is also associated with low emotional intelligence (EI), which is the ability to manage your own emotions and understand the emotions of people around you. Dad had very low EI, and I wonder whether this might have been partly caused by genetic factors. Elements of Dad's behaviour resembled autism, including finding it hard to understand how other people felt, getting very anxious in social situations, seeming blunt, rude or not interested in other people without meaning to, finding it tough to say how he felt, avoiding eye contact - he struggled to look me in the eye - getting too close to people physically, and having a passionate interest in particular things - for Dad this was the Law. I'm not saying that Dad was autistic, but I do believe that he had many of its typical characteristics, which may have been genetically caused.

Another thing that contributed to Dad's difficulty with empathy and intimacy was simply the era in which he was born. Dad was born in 1935, and in Australia, at least from the 1930s to the 1970s and perhaps beyond, the culture and social norms that defined how men and women behaved and interacted dictated that men were the head of the household and sole provider, while women were expected to be the homemakers who cared for the children. While the involvement of individual fathers in parenting varied considerably, most men were still the providers.

Looking at research from the 1950s, it was common for a man to spend most of his time working away from his family, because it was accepted that most men were not emotionally able to raise their children. So it was better for men to come back with the iron fist at the end of the day, and women reinforced this with "wait till your father comes home." Apparently, this was the way it was meant to be. A man didn't need any warmth or physical contact apart from sex, and he needed fewer hugs and kisses and was not outwardly affectionate. Back then, men were not involved in any significant way in the pregnancy, birth, breastfeeding or any day-to-day, hands-on raising of children. A man didn't even go with his wife to hospital and wasn't allowed in the labour ward during the birth. His duty was to teach children by example to be reliable, think rationally, and develop a strong work ethic. He was protective of his wife and children in a physical way, but not emotionally.

It's interesting to note that Dad was one of the Silent Generation – born between 1928 and 1945, the Great Depression to the end of World War II - and thrifty because there was rationing and economic uncertainty. They were also respectful of authority, and usually had the same job for their entire working life. They were faithful to their beliefs, relationships, and families, and they valued stability, so they didn't question the status quo or the norms of their times. They were also determined to survive with grit and strength. When I reflect that both my parents were born then, it helps me understand the power of the cultural and social norms and expectations in their behaviour and parenting approach. Dad was just doing what was expected of him, nothing more and nothing less.

Dad passed away about three years ago in 2021. By then I had built a good relationship with him. I had found a way to accept him for who he was, and to know that he did love me but couldn't say or show it the way that I had wanted as a child and young man. Dad never hugged me or expressed any physical or verbal affection. It took until I was about 40, and years of study and being a psychologist, to work out where my own strong need for approval came from, and how to let it go. I recently heard a lovely quote by Soren Kierkegaard: "Life can only be understood backwards, but it must be lived forwards." This has helped me understand my relationship with my father.

For years I did not understand why I needed to seek approval constantly, why I did many things just to be loved. My need for approval was strong, because in my eyes my father never approved of me. He was the one person that I wanted approval from, but it was too hard for him to show it. Eventually, after years of self-reflection, I realised that he did love me, but he couldn't show it in the important ways that I needed. He was enormously proud of the person I had become, but he couldn't say so. He cared for me deeply but couldn't physically show it. When I began to look for signs of this, they were there. He wanted to spend time with me. We played scrabble together regularly in his last few years. We had dinner together. He was interested in my career and my family. I came to accept all his small gestures and means of telling me he was proud of me. I also realised that I was enough; I didn't need his approval. I was a good person without needing my father to tell me so. I still wanted his approval, but no longer needed it. This made a fundamental difference to me, and helped me to improve my self-worth and, simultaneously, my relationship with Dad.

As I reflect on this, I also consider how it must have been for Craig and Q. I was always the golden child. I was invited to dinner with Dad. I was brought out by Dad to play tennis with his legal friends when I was a teenager and shown off. I was reasonably academically successful. Craig and Q were not shown even this type of love and affection, and I know they felt quite empty.

Dad's life is a good example of how some people can have a mental illness and yet still function well and lead a reasonably satisfying and fulfilling life. He was outstandingly successful in his chosen career, and I am sure his achievements sustained his wellbeing and enhanced his sense of purpose and the meaning of his life. He achieved many fine things, despite his mental illness, and that is truly inspiring.

Q – Break-down #1

After I went to the US to play tennis at college, Q was on his own and had to organise himself. This was not his strength. Given that he was a very good baseline tennis player, he decided to go to Spain to play the satellite circuit on clay courts. For those who are not tennis nuts like me, clay courts are a lot slower than other surfaces, therefore it is more difficult to be aggressive and hit winners. They do not suit players who like to come to the net and hit volleys, which was good for Q, because he was a strong baseline player with a lot of patience, who could rally all day from the back of the court. He travelled to Spain with our good mate Ian Peter-Budge.

Q and Ian left Melbourne and arrived in Barcelona exhausted from the marathon journey with multiple stopovers. They knew that they had to get a train to a place called Lerida. This was in the days before the Internet, and they had looked it up on the map. One way or another, they made their way to the train station from the airport in Barcelona and found the right train, but it was late evening, and it was dark. The train stopped at a station that had a sign 'Lleida'. Unbeknown to Q and Ian, this was the Spanish spelling of the town they were looking for - Lerida was the English spelling - and they didn't get off.

They eventually realised their mistake and got off at the next stop, but this was a long way away. They assumed a train would come past soon going back in the other direction and planned on taking that. They waited for a couple of hours. It was already 11pm when they arrived at this unknown station in a very small town in the middle of nowhere in

Spain, and eventually at about 1:30am a freight train approached. It didn't stop, but it was travelling very slowly and had an open carriage, so Q said "Let's run and jump on." Without thinking, they grabbed their tennis gear and bags and ran as fast as they could, caught up with the train, and reached the open carriage, like you see people doing in old Westerns. They threw their gear onto the moving train and hoisted themselves up and onto the carriage. The floor was hard, so they lay down on top of their bags nervously and tried to stay out of sight so as not to attract any attention.

Not long afterwards, the freight train stopped at Lleida. Q and Ian got off, worried that railway inspectors would find them, and they would be in trouble. They made their way from the station over a side fence quietly and quickly at about 2am, but now that they had arrived, they had another decision to make: the Satellite Tournament was starting at nine, and they needed to be as fresh as possible. This was becoming unlikely, given what had just happened, and Q was concerned about money. He wanted his money to last for the three months they planned on travelling together, and said "Why don't we just save our money and sleep outside somewhere?" Ian didn't like the idea and replied, "We need some sleep and a warm shower at least." They had been travelling for a long time just to get here. Eventually Ian's good sense prevailed, and they found a very cheap hotel for a few hours' sleep and a shower, but unfortunately, when they woke up after three or four hours and turned on the taps, there was no hot water and so they had to put up with a cold shower.

They both got dressed in their tennis gear and made it to the Lleida Tennis Club by nine, only to be told that they were a day late and the tournament had started the day before. Somehow, they had miscalculated and got the dates wrong. When you play a Satellite Circuit, there are generally four tournaments in a row. The best players then play off in a Masters' event in the fifth week. However, if you miss the first week of the circuit you can't usually play the rest of the events.

This was devastating for Q and Ian, who decided to practise hard and get used to the Spanish clay courts. They also enquired about the next tournament and worked out that they probably could play the next week's event but would not be eligible for the Masters if they got that far, but Ian noticed after a few days that Q had changed. He said "I need my space," and kept going off to Barcelona on his own. Gradually he practised less and wanted more time to himself, so after about ten days of moving from one hotel to another together, Ian played a practice session with another tennis player and noticed Q was not around. When he hadn't seen Q for nearly a day, he became worried.

Ian walked all around Barcelona looking for Q but couldn't find him, and after a few days he contacted his mother and told her he was concerned. Ian's mum called my mother, who told her Q wasn't coping and was on his way home. At least that reassured Ian, as he had had visions of Q wandering around Spain by himself. A few days later, Ian found out from his mother that Q was "at home in Australia in bed" and hadn't coped well with the stress of the trip. Ian felt that Q had not been his normal self, and that something had flipped in his mind. He used to want to practise all the time, but those last few days in Spain he hadn't wanted to train and had been very anxious. Everything that could have gone wrong, did go wrong, and for a young 17-year-old like Q it was just too much.

Then there was the Chernobyl disaster in Ukraine on 26 April 1986. The explosion caused at least five percent of the radioactive reactor core to be released into the environment with the deposition of radioactive materials in many parts of Europe. Two Chernobyl plant workers died on the night, and a further 28 people within a few weeks due to acute radiation caused by the explosion. Approximately 350,000 people had to be evacuated.

Q told us that he was so worried about the radiation that he needed to come home, but while I have no doubt that this contributed to his anxiety, it was far from the full story. His stress levels were very high, and I was not there to help organise things and support him off-court to ensure he could perform well. I don't know if this had an impact on his mental state, but clearly, he was not managing, and the trip was not going to plan. In his panic, he bought a plane ticket home, despite already having one. Q was supposed to be playing tennis tournaments in Spain for three months, but somehow with Mum's help he made his way to London, and from there back to Sydney. He arrived in Sydney without any money and called Mum to ask for help to get to Melbourne. She managed to organise the ticket, which in those days was harder without the Internet and the simplicity of remote transactions.

When Q arrived home, he realised that he was not well mentally and went to Hampton Medical Clinic where he saw a general practitioner.

I have no idea why Mum didn't take him - it seems strange to me. The doctor didn't do much - he didn't even put Q on medication. Perhaps Q didn't tell him the full story. At this point, all we knew was that Q had had a 'breakdown'. This was not a formal diagnosis of any kind, but rather a term we all used to try to understand what was happening. We tended to use terms like nervous breakdown to describe how stress and anxiety built up to a significant impact on someone's life and became physically and emotionally overwhelming so that they could no longer carry out basic daily tasks and activities. It is not a medical term, but used when mental health attention and support are necessary.

Diagnosis and the early years

Between Q's first nervous breakdown in May and November 1986, he tried to continue playing tennis back in Australia. I had returned from the US in September, and Q and I trained together, but his behaviour was increasingly erratic, and he had suddenly become religious. We were not a religious family, and in fact Mum was a staunch atheist as her father had been. There was no grey in it for Mum - she was certain that when you die your body is under the ground and your soul or spirit ceases to exist. Q started carrying a bible around with him and read it regularly. He shunned anything he considered materialistic, and this all led to his smashing our entire home with an axe.

Following this traumatic episode, Q stayed in Larundel Mental Asylum for several months. It was all new to us, scary and frightening, and so I can only imagine how terrifying it must have been for Q. It was a locked ward - his freedom had been taken away. Although Q looked bad, it was hard to compare my brother to all the other patients walking around like zombies. The medication caused awful side effects like stiff limbs, shuffling, and jiggling from side to side, which we used to call the Modecate Shuffle. This was the first time we were told he had schizophrenia.

Understanding Schizophrenia

Schizophrenia is a terribly misunderstood term. My family have all been frustrated over the years by hearing people use the term inappropriately to mean split personality or Jekyll and Hyde or something similar. Or they refer to someone as being a schizophrenic. This is also wrong. The person is a human being with an illness called schizophrenia. They are not the illness. Schizophrenia is a serious mental disorder in which people interpret reality abnormally. They may have some combination of hallucinations, delusions, and extremely disordered thinking and behaviour that impairs their daily functioning. Sadly, Q had all these symptoms, and they usually require lifelong treatment. They have either continuous or relapsing episodes of psychosis. Q had continuous psychosis over nearly 35 years with no improvement between the relapses. Occasionally the psychosis was less severe, but it never went away. Psychosis is a condition of the mind that results in difficulties determining what is real and what is not. Sometimes people with schizophrenia withdraw socially and have a flat affect, and at times Q had both these symptoms. About 0.3 to 0.7% of people are diagnosed with schizophrenia during their lifetime. Globally, about 24 million people have the illness.

In the past, schizophrenia was divided into five subtypes: paranoid, catatonic, disorganised, residual, and undifferentiated. However, these classifications are not used as frequently today by experts, because individuals with schizophrenia often experience overlapping symptoms throughout their lives and so sub-categories are less useful. Nonetheless, it is helpful to appreciate and recognise the different types to understand that the illness can manifest in diverse ways. Catatonic schizophrenia is characterised by either excessive or decreased movement. Individuals with this type may not react to certain stimuli and may make odd movements or experience extreme rigidity of the limbs. Disorganised schizophrenia (also known as hebephrenic schizophrenia) has disorganised behaviours and nonsensical speech. Other symptoms include flat affect, inappropriate emotional and facial reactions, disorganised thinking, and difficulty with daily tasks. Residual schizophrenia is where the individual previously had symptoms such as delusions and hallucinations, but no longer experiences these, yet still shows symptoms such as flat affect, psychomotor difficulties, and disturbed speech. Undifferentiated schizophrenia describes symptoms fitting into more than one subtype, such as delusions and catatonic behaviour.

Scientists still don't know exactly what causes schizophrenia, but contributing factors are likely to include genetic, physical, psychological, and environmental aspects. Schizophrenia runs in families, but no single gene is thought to be responsible. It is likely that a combination of genes makes people more vulnerable to the condition, and the best estimates of the heritability of schizophrenia are that 70-80% of the individual differences in risk of the illness are associated with genetics. The greatest risk factor (6.5%) is having a first-degree relative with the disease. More than 40% of identical twins of those with schizophrenia have the illness too. If one parent is affected the risk is about 13%, and if both have it the risk is 50%.

Studies have shown there are subtle differences in the brain structure of those with schizophrenia, which suggests the illness may partly be a disorder of the brain. Neurotransmitters are chemicals that carry messages between brain cells, and it is thought that people with schizophrenia may have different numbers of specific neurotransmitters in their brains. The strongest link is with the chemical dopamine. Dopamine plays a role in how we feel pleasure and is a big part of our unique human ability to think and plan. It helps us strive, focus, and find things interesting, and too much or too little may lead to a vast range of health issues. Too little dopamine contributes significantly to Parkinson's disease, and it is thought that people with schizophrenia have too much dopamine. Therefore, patients are given medication to help reduce the amount of dopamine in their brains, which helps reduce the symptoms. The fact that this type of medicine generally works suggests that dopamine plays a role in the development of schizophrenia.

Research shows that people who develop schizophrenia are more likely to have experienced complications before and during birth, such as a low birthweight, premature labour, or lack of oxygen, and these may play some minor role, but the main psychological trigger of schizophrenia is stressful life events, such as bereavement, divorce, or physical, sexual or emotional abuse. Although these do not actually cause schizophrenia, they can trigger its development. Schizophrenia may lie dormant in some people and never rear its ugly head, but stressful events can trigger it in others, normally between the ages of 17 and 25.

From an environmental perspective, childhood traumas, toxic stress, and chronic trauma with significant negative life events contribute to the illness. Research shows that those with a genetic predisposition towards developing schizophrenia are more vulnerable to the effects of environmental risk factors, and substance abuse is also a major contributing factor. About half those with schizophrenia use recreational drugs, including alcohol, tobacco and cannabis, excessively, and use of stimulants such as amphetamines and cocaine may lead to temporary psychosis. Drugs are habitually used as coping mechanisms, and cannabis use may be a contributing factor in the development of schizophrenia, potentially increasing the risks for those already susceptible. Cannabis use in the presence of other risk factors may double the rate of contracting the disease.

Q had never used cannabis before developing schizophrenia. He was extremely fit, healthy, and disciplined. Unlike me, he rarely drank alcohol and didn't smoke cigarettes, although later in life he used and sometimes abused these drugs as a coping mechanism. However, substances had no role in Q developing the illness. My view, having reviewed a lot of the literature over the years, is that Q had a strong genetic predisposition towards schizophrenia: Nana probably had the disease to a mild degree. Dad had bipolar disorder. Aunty Joan had severe depression and, I suspect, also undiagnosed schizophrenia. Mental health issues were on Dad's side of the family.

When Q experienced numerous serious disturbances, the cumulative stress pushed him over the edge and triggered schizophrenia:

the combination of stressors with him trying to make it on the world tennis tour as a 17-year-old without anyone to help him navigate this complex world, the distressing experience in Spain, finding Nana lying on the ground in a pool of her own blood, and of course our parents going through a highly charged and emotional separation and divorce. All these events happened within a 12-month period, and I also believe that Q had not developed strong foundational skills in communication and organisation. He was a funny, quirky, cheeky kid - very likeable, but messy and disorganised, and not a good or clear communicator, and I believe that this was another contributing factor, because when he was going through all these extreme challenges, he did not have the resources to cope with the demands that life was throwing at him. This was compounded by the fact that he clearly had a strong genetic predisposition towards the illness.

Schizophrenia has what are termed positive and negative symptoms. The positive symptoms (not really very positive, if you ask me) are those present during a psychotic episode such as delusions, hallucinations, and disorganised thoughts and speech. Most commonly, the hallucinations are auditory (hearing voices) but can also involve changes to other senses such as taste, sight, smell, and touch. Delusions are usually bizarre or persecutory in nature, and interestingly there appears to be too much dopamine in certain parts of the brain that relate to hallucinations and delusions. Q certainly had many of these throughout his life. Distortions of self-experience, such as feeling others can hear one's thoughts, are common. Q thought he had telepathic abilities. Typically, the positive symptoms respond well to medication, but unfortunately for Q the medications only served to reduce the severity of his hallucinations and delusions, and never to eradicate them.

The negative symptoms include deficits of normal emotional responses. These could be blunt affect, where there are flat expressions - monotone, alogia leading to poverty of speech, anhedonia, which is an inability to feel pleasure, asociality – the lack of desire to form relationships, and avolition – the lack of motivation and apathy. Research suggests that dopamine is lacking in different parts of the brain relating to these negative symptoms. I think Q had the blunt affect symptom and avolition, but I don't recall him suffering from the other three symptoms. Apathy is the most common of these for about 50 percent of those suffering from schizophrenia, and it is related to disrupted cognitive processing, affecting memory and planning.

Frequently people with a mental illness have what is known as dual diagnosis, and Q was also diagnosed with schizoaffective disorder. This is where there are substantial symptoms of a mood disorder too, alongside psychotic symptoms. He also had bipolar disorder - periods of depression and periods of abnormally elevated mood, as I described in relation to my father. Management of Q's illnesses was challenging, because medication to help with one symptom would often react badly with another. This is assuming he was taking his medication, which often he did not.

The primary treatment of schizophrenia is antipsychotic medications combined with psychosocial interventions such as cognitive behavioural therapy, family therapy, and social support. However, Q never had any talking therapy of any kind, and social support was not great until the National Disability Insurance Scheme (NDIS) came along in the latter part of his life. The main antipsychotic drugs known as dopamine antagonists block the effects of the neurotransmitter dopamine. More recent medications also seek to block another neurotransmitter called serotonin. Sometimes Q accepted that he had an illness, however mostly he denied it. This is the case for about 30-50% of people with schizophrenia. He was rarely disciplined about taking his medication, and so for years he would relapse badly and then spend months in the psychiatric ward until he had improved enough to go home. Eventually he had to be put on long-acting injections, which helped a lot, but Q hated them because they made him drowsy, and he ended up going to bed within an hour or two of the injection, which was usually at 3-4pm.

Episodes

In the first five to ten years, Q had many traumatic and sometimes bizarre episodes. Mum's father Pa died in 1988. Q was at Larundel, and we brought him out for the day to attend Pa's funeral. Q was 19 years old at this point and had been dealing with his illness for two years. It was clearly a very emotional day for Mum. As the funeral was about to begin, we noticed that Q had zinc cream all over his face and had climbed a tree and refused to come inside the chapel. Mum is very stoic, and she did not want to let this affect her grieving for her father. The funeral began, and it was proceeding as you would expect. Mum was giving her eulogy as Q walked in barefoot and lay down on his stomach in the middle of the aisle, looking up at Mum with his face in his hands. Mum saw this while she was in the middle of her passionate speech about her father, and she slowed down, paused, and then took a deep breath and continued reading her speech as if nothing were happening. Yvette and I were sitting next to each other, holding hands and crying quietly. Q was spoiling Mum's grieving for her father, and I felt terrible for her, but didn't know what to do. It was still early days for us, and we were yet to fully comprehend the gravity of what had happened to our brother. He was psychotic, and not in control of his mind or his actions.

When the funeral was over, we all drove back to Mum's mother's house for the wake, but we couldn't find Q. We searched for several hours, but he had disappeared without a trace. Then Mum received a phone call from the team at Larundel saying he was back there. They told us that he had left the funeral and got on a bus, stripped naked, and caused a few problems for other passengers. The police were called, and they took him to Larundel.

Although back then the police were not trained very well to manage people like Q with severe mental illness, they often did a fine job and showed genuine compassion, and Mum was grateful for the role the police played in this disturbing event. I still have a copy of her letter to the 'Officer in Charge' at the Brighton Police Station dated 23.07.1988. She wrote:

> "Last Wednesday night, my son Q, who suffers from schizophrenia, had a very nasty attack and had to be sent to Larundel. I would like you to know how pleased I and the rest of my family were with the way your people handled Q at home here, during our visit to Sandringham Hospital and finally to Larundel. Many thanks for your assistance, which was greatly appreciated."

I recall one occasion when Q had become horribly aggressive and violent. This was highly unusual for Q as he was usually a very soft, easy-going and gentle person, not hostile at all, and he only became belligerent when he had delusions and/or hallucinations. We could always see it in Q's eyes when he was psychotic. On numerous occasions his psychosis was associated with paranoia.

I walked into our home in Montclair Ave, Brighton, once and Q was naked. His eyes were wild, and he was yelling. I couldn't understand what he was saying, and I can't recall who called for help, however before I knew it no fewer than nine police cars arrived. It was like a scene from a low-budget police movie with the flashing lights illuminating the night. Q was on the stairs inside, and when the police came in, he became more agitated and hostile. Four policemen threw him on the ground and held him down on the bottom few steps of the house. I watched with horror as they proceeded to put a straitjacket on him. He was fighting all the way, spitting and angry. They took him to one of the divvy vans and one of the policemen asked if I wanted to sit in the back of the divvy van with him. I said yes and got in and tried to calm him down as well as to hold him steady and upright as we rolled around in the back of the van, with Q in a very awkward position in the straitjacket. He was taken back to Larundel, where he spent many months once again.

These episodes were traumatic for us all, but Q suffered the most. By then he had stopped playing tennis and started smoking cigarettes. Most patients in psychiatric hospitals smoke cigarettes, and Q experimented with other drugs too. He smoked marijuana, although luckily this didn't become a regular thing for him. On one occasion a friend injected Q with heroin, and unfortunately, he contracted hepatitis C, an illness that causes inflammation of the liver and is spread through contact with infected blood, usually through an injection where needles are shared. Most infections are asymptomatic and don't lead to a life-threatening disease. Symptoms include fever, fatigue, loss of appetite, nausea, abdominal pain, dark urine, and yellowing of the skin or eyes, and there is a 15-30% chance of developing cirrhosis of the liver within 20 years. With the overlap of his mental illness, it was hard to tell what was causing his symptoms. He did suffer from abdominal pain, difficulties urinating at times, and jaundice. Years afterwards he was able to take a direct-acting antiviral medicine, and eventually he was cured.

Later, Q would self-medicate with Advil tablets. Advil is meant to be used as an anti-inflammatory drug to reduce pain or fever, but he took it because it gave him a bit of a high and he liked the feeling. This is a little strange because it is meant to have the opposite effect and can cause drowsiness as well as terrible side effects including stomach bleeding, liver problems, nausea, dark urine, jaundice, and kidney problems, which meant it was difficult for us to tell if the hepatitis C was affecting him or the Advil. Of course, when we asked him if he had taken any Advil, he would usually deny it. Q didn't drink much alcohol but occasionally he would skull five or six cans of beer very quickly with the aim of getting drunk fast. I was grateful that he didn't do that regularly.

Schizophrenia and cigarettes

It was totally understandable that Q tried to find drugs that made him feel better. I was pleased that most of the drugs he tried didn't lead to addiction, as he would have had an additional problem of battling schizophrenia, bipolar disorder, and drugs. However, he did become addicted to cigarettes, which caused grave problems later in life. This is so common that it is very unusual for patients with schizophrenia not to smoke. One study by Kelly and McCreadie, published by Cambridge University Press in 2018, reported the prevalence to be 88%, nearly three times the rate in the general population, and higher than the elevated rates of smoking in patients with other psychiatric illnesses. Regrettably, the proportion of those who quit is much lower than in the general population too. It has been recognised for many years that patients with schizophrenia smoke to excess, and Q smoked anywhere from 30-60 cigarettes a day for many years once he had started. However, while 90% of people with schizophrenia start smoking before their illness begins, Q had never smoked. This excessive smoking causes many physical health problems, and the most common causes of death for people with schizophrenia are cardiovascular and respiratory disease, both smoking related, and Q's physical health issues were related to both of these. There are many possible reasons why so many people with schizophrenia smoke excessively. One suggestion is that it is a form of self-medication with nicotine, which may increase dopamine release in the pre-frontal cortex and alleviate the positive and negative symptoms. Patients often report that it helps them "relax and calm down", and research also suggests that genetic factors may predispose individuals to developing both schizophrenia and nicotine addiction. Most work in this area has focused on the dopamine receptor system in the brain, but I also believe that, once Q entered the mental health system, he was medicated to the point where he slowed down a great deal, and was sitting around with other patients, all of whom were smoking, so that this environment made it almost impossible not to smoke. Regardless of the contributing factors, Q smoked to excess for many years with serious consequences.

Can things get any worse?

By 1993, Yvette was living away from home and Q had moved out too, because Mum was not able to cope with him and had asked him to move. He shared a house in Malvern for a few years, and was attending the Malvern Clinic, which is a beautiful big building with lovely gardens, a tranquil place for patients with mental illness to come and spend time and get the social support they desperately need. Q had been dealing with his illness for six or seven years by this time, and it was beginning to take a significant toll on him. He hated his life, and was going through another psychotic episode in September 1993, although I didn't know it then. I was engaged to my wife Lynne, and we had started a two-year trip around the world. We spent a few months travelling around the US, and after a couple of weeks in Hawaii we flew to Seattle, where we bought a 1974 Dodge van, fully equipped with a fridge, sink, stove, bed, and a huge loudspeaker to play our music at any volume we wanted. Living the dream, we travelled down the West Coast of America, taking in the beautiful beaches in Northern California and the gorgeous redwood forests. After reaching Southern California, we headed east through Las Vegas, the Grand Canyon, Texas, and New Orleans before making it over to Florida on the southern part of the East Coast. We eventually went up to New York, where we worked for three months. I was a tennis coach on Fire Island, where wealthy New Yorkers would come for a month at a time with their families over the summer holidays, and Lynne was head of housekeeping at a large hotel right on the beach, only metres from the water. After this, we drove north up to Canada, where we spent time in Quebec and Montreal before heading towards Toronto.

Lynne and I were staying at a campground in our van on the outskirts of a small city in Ontario called Kingston. I recall that it was around eight or nine in the morning, and we were still in bed, just waking to a new day in paradise, when the silence was shattered by a thumping fist on the door of our van. I opened the door to an older man whom we knew of through Dad but had never met. He lived in Kingston, and said "Your mother has been trying to find you and wants you to call her immediately."

My heart sank. I knew in my gut that it would be about Q. We thanked him, got dressed and quickly made our way to a telephone booth – this was in the days before mobile phones. Lynne and I crowded into the small telephone box and called Mum. I was not sure what to expect, but I knew it must be bad if Mum had tracked me down in the middle of nowhere. She answered the phone. My heart was pounding, both wanting and not wanting to know what had happened. Mum came straight out with it, and said "Q has been in an accident. He has lost both his legs." I couldn't stand up. I dropped the phone and fell inside the cramped telephone box. Lynne picked it up and listened to the rest of the story. Q was at the Alfred Hospital in the Intensive Care Unit. He was alive, but unconscious and in a coma. He might not make it.

Lynne was amazing. She realised I was in a state of shock, and so she took control and organised our immediate return home. We made our way to the nearest airport, purchased tickets, left our van in Canada with a friend, Paul, not knowing if we would be coming back, and began the longest of trips home to Australia.

We heard the full story when we arrived. On Tuesday, 28 September 1993, Q was at Mum's house, and Mum was on the phone trying to get a bed for him at one of the psychiatric hospitals in Melbourne because he was clearly going downhill fast. There was a shortage of hospital beds in psychiatric wards in Melbourne at the time, which was not unusual. Our home in Montclair Avenue backed onto a train line. We had become used to the noise of the trains, and usually blocked it out and didn't really hear them. Mum looked up and saw several policemen walking up our driveway towards her. Immediately and instinctively, she knew what had happened. Q had tried to commit suicide by lying on the train tracks, but in his delusional state he got it all wrong and lay on the wrong tracks, so the train sliced through his legs and severed them both just below his knees. I later discovered that he had smoked marijuana a few days prior to this, and that may have triggered his psychosis, although we will never know. Q later described how he saw a policeman holding up his leg with his shoe on it. Somehow, he was lucid enough to respond to the police, but bizarrely he told them his name was Craig Fricke and he gave Craig's date of birth. He must have given them Mum's address too.

Yvette and her husband Glenn were living in Keysborough, about 30 minutes away, at the time. Yvette remembers that she had thought about visiting Q in Malvern, also about 30 minutes away, on her way home from work, but decided not to because she was going to see another friend, Debbie. So, Yvette was at Debbie's house, and Glenn was at home and had listened to a couple of messages on the answering machine. He called Yvette at Debbie's and said "Your mum and dad have left messages for you; Q has been in an accident, but they wouldn't say any more. He is in Intensive Care at the Alfred." Glenn immediately picked Yvette up and drove to the hospital. When they walked into the ICU area, Mum was sitting outside in a little waiting room. They hugged and cried as Mum explained what had happened. Q was in surgery, and they were told it would be a long time, so they went home. Q was in surgery for 14 hours. They took the skin from the soles of his feet, which the policeman had found and taken to the hospital and connected them up to the ends of his legs, which were now stumps just under his knees. The surgeons explained that this was because the skin on the soles of the feet is the toughest, and copes best with the pressure of wearing prosthetic legs.

After the surgery, Yvette and Mum went back to the hospital to see Q. Yvette walked into the ICU and recalls having to use hand sanitizer - COVID recently brought these memories back for her. Q was unconscious and on life support. He had a tube in his mouth, and later they did a tracheostomy, so a tube was inserted into his neck to help oxygen reach his lungs by creating an opening into his windpipe. Yvette looked at Q and at the white hospital blankets, and then she saw the outline where his legs ended. She had to sit down, because otherwise she knew she was going to pass out. She noticed Q was puffy, and yellow in colour. He had a small scratch on his shoulder but was otherwise untouched apart from losing his legs. This was the first of her daily visits to see Q in hospital.

Later Yvette drove to the Gardenvale police station. She was concerned about the mental wellbeing of the train driver and asked for a message to be sent telling him that Q was alive. At the time we didn't know the statistics, however we had heard that this was not uncommon, and it must be a horrendous experience for train drivers to witness and not be able to do anything about it. I have since found out from a report by the TrackSafe Foundation that between 2016 and 2021 roughly 75 people died per year by suicide across Australia's rail network. Only one person in four who attempt suicide this way survives, and Q was one of those. I'm not sure if that was a good thing. Three quarters of those who died were young men, with 42% aged under 30. So, Yvette did the right thing by telling the police, and hopefully her message was passed on to the train driver.

After a long couple of days making our way home, Lynne and I went to see Q. He was unconscious and hooked up to all sorts of tubes and monitors measuring his vital health information to keep him alive. Initially we were not sure if he was going to survive. I visited him every day. He was in ICU for about a month. Each time he woke up, he was extremely angry. He didn't want to be alive. He kept trying to jump out of bed and succeeded on several occasions. To stop him, the doctors had given him "enough medication to kill a horse" we were told, but he was so strong and determined that they had to strap him to the bed. This was awfully painful to see as well. He didn't want to be alive, and was angry with himself for having made himself a cripple (as he used to say). The skin from the soles of his feet didn't take due to his jumping out of bed, and the doctors eventually had to operate again. They took a skin flap from along the side of his back, which they used to adhere to his leg stumps, and finally this worked and the bottom of his stumps began to heal.

Q was moved from the ICU to another ward that was still thorough and rigorous in its procedures for someone with his complex issues. The hospital had trouble dealing with Q's behaviour because he had the double problem of substantial physical and psychological issues. He remained very aggressive for several months.

One day Yvette went to visit him. It was a beautiful sunny day, and there was a nice warm, light area where they went to have a chat. They were both lying on the grass, having a lovely conversation, when totally out of the blue Q punched her hard in the face. She never saw it coming. She was shocked and physically hurt. He had split her lip open, and it was bleeding profusely. Yvette ran inside the hospital and found a nurse. Luckily, they were able to help her immediately. It was so bizarre, and such unusually aggressive behaviour from Q. Over the years, Q apologised for punching Yvette many times. We're still not sure what kind of delusion or hallucination caused it.

The hospital organised something called a 'Craig bed', which is a padded bed with a mattress on the floor and padded sides of about 70 centimetres in height. It was like a little prison cell. At one stage he tried to set himself on fire by lighting the bed sheets. He had burns on his stomach, and they put three psychiatric nurses on rotation 24 hours a day, seven days a week, for three months. He was too physically ill for the psychiatric ward, and too mentally unwell for the general ward.

I witnessed this daily for several months, and it affected my own mental health badly. I kept thinking that I didn't want him to live. I felt so torn and helpless, and it was intensely painful to watch my little brother. He was no longer the brother that I had grown up with. He hated himself and his life and had even messed up trying to kill himself. He had now made his life worse and would have to be in a wheelchair for the rest of his life. I felt guilty for wanting him to die, but I also knew life was unbearably sad and distressing for him. I knew that he didn't want to live, and I wanted him to find peace.

He eventually recovered although never fully. We had many family meetings with staff at the Alfred Hospital. He was getting sores sitting in the wheelchair all day, which he wasn't used to. If you were a psychiatric patient, they had a rule that you had to be up and about each day, and couldn't stay in bed, but he needed to lie down to have a break from the wheelchair. The Alfred hospital was not equipped to cope with the double disability of being a psychiatric patient and a double-leg amputee, but despite the great difficulties they had taking care of Q, they did an incredible job overall and Mum wanted to thank them as best she could. In a letter to the hospital Board of Management on 29.06.1994, she wrote:

> "Tomorrow, nine months and two days after his attempted suicide, in which Q lost his legs just below the knee, he will leave your fine hospital. This letter is expressly written to show my family's gratitude to the surgeons for their untiring efforts to save Q's life. I would appreciate it if the wonderful doctors could be told Q is

going to Caulfield Hospital tomorrow to be rehabilitated. He has had prosthetics fitted. I bought him a pair of shoes yesterday and commented he should be with me to choose them, and he said 'What for, Mum? I haven't got any feet,' and we both laughed, so we've all come a long way in nine months.

… "The Alfred has become like Q's home, and he is a little nervous now about leaving, but he and his family will never forget the staff of the Alfred – the intensive care staff were wonderful also."

Q moved to Caulfield Hospital where he stayed for six months. Caulfield Hospital was set up much better for rehabilitation, and slowly he began to improve. After he came home and was trying to adjust to life without his legs, he wrote a letter to Mum that gives some insight into his social challenges:

"I think going out in public like restaurants or shopping is hard because children or people ask about my amputations. They usually ask how did you lose your legs? So, I'd rather stay with friends at their house and eat and drink there. But in the future to avoid these questions I'm going to try to walk on prosthetics."

Sadly, he was never able to walk on his prosthetic legs, because he was not able to practise regularly and slowly build up the toughness in the skin at the base of his amputations. He kept overdoing it and bleeding, and then couldn't continue for many months, so he spent most of his time in a wheelchair.

It was intriguing to observe how people responded differently to Q after he lost his legs compared to losing his mind when he was first diagnosed with schizophrenia. After news spread about his 'accident' (which we continue to call it even though it was a suicide attempt and not an accident), people showed incredible empathy and support. We received an amazing number of bunches of flowers with beautifully written personal cards that demonstrated affection and compassion. It was truly humbling to feel the love from so many friends and family. Yet when Q had gone into Larundel following his first diagnosis and major episode, we got nothing. Gradually over the years, Q lost his friends. Some of them let go immediately, others over time. I observed that people feel comfortable and know how to respond when someone has a major physical illness or injury by sending flowers and a nice card but are awkward and uncomfortable about responding to serious mental illness. I'm sure that those same people cared and felt concerned, but they lacked the skills and capabilities to respond. It is not really a normal part of our society yet, despite the high rate of mental health issues. I hope we can improve this. The saddest part of this story is that Q's mental health issues were always far worse and had more negative impact on his life than the loss of his legs.

On another sad note, Mum had to sell her beloved home in Brighton after this ordeal. She found the memory too traumatic, and continually hearing the train go past was simply too much to bear. She left only four months after Q's suicide attempt.

Conversations with people with mental illness

—

Why is it so hard for people to talk openly about mental illness? There is still a lot of stigma, prejudice, and discrimination, often subtle and not overt, and people with mental health concerns find it difficult to explain even to their closest friends how they feel. In many relationships, not enough space is given to vulnerable conversations. People are not able to talk about mental illness because the feelings are overwhelming. Sometimes they feel weak if they talk about their mental health challenges, and in addition when they do find the courage to say something, a frequent response is "don't worry" or "it will be fine" or another comment aimed at making the discomfort go away. Unfortunately, this only leads to them feeling dismissed, and not having a safe space to share their thoughts and feelings. Sometimes symptoms of anxiety and depression are oversimplified and labelled as stress or sensitivity, which makes it difficult for them to talk about complex suicidal thoughts or self-harm.

This is why it is hard for people with a mental illness to talk about it, but why is it difficult for other people to raise the issue? One reason is that they don't know what to say. Here are some tips: asking open-ended questions helps. For example, say something like "I've noticed you haven't been yourself lately – is everything OK?" Sometimes people worry that they won't know what to say if the person says they are not OK. The key is to listen, and not to try to solve the problem. To show active listening, you need to use micro-communication skills such as reflective listening, summarising or paraphrasing to encourage the person to keep talking and to demonstrate that you are listening. The other person feels heard, and most of the time this is the key goal and helps them feel they are not alone. As you listen, avoid judgemental language and don't minimise their feelings with comments like "It will pass" or "It will be OK." Afterwards, you may want to help them do some research and work out what the next step should be, such as making an appointment with their doctor to get help. Don't force this, because they may not be ready to seek help, so be available to talk again until they are ready.

To find out more about how to have conversations about mental health issues, I suggest you look at a non-profit suicide prevention and mental illness organisation called R U OK? They were founded in 2009 by Gavin Larkin, and the work they do revolves around the slogan "R U OK?" where they advocate for people to have conversations. They run an annual R U OK? Day in September each year, encouraging people to connect with those who have emotional insecurity, address social isolation, and promote community cohesiveness. Sadly, Gavin Larkin passed away in 2011 of cancer, however his family have continued the great work he began. R U OK? Day has been successful in raising awareness about mental health issues and suicide, and in helping people to begin to talk about these challenges, however it has also been criticised for being too superficial and simplistic. I personally feel that their work has been a wonderful start to increasing the conversations we all have about mental health, and we need to build on it, to go deeper, and to have better conversations. We need to learn how to respond after we ask "Are you OK?" We need to find ways to be OK ourselves with the discomfort associated with such conversations, and just sit with those uncomfortable states for a little bit longer so that people can truly feel heard and understood, ultimately leading to reduced isolation and pain. Furthermore, we need to build habits and social norms around having these conversations more regularly and not just on one day in September each year. This needs to become a part of our 'normal' conversations.

Long-term patterns

Over the years following Q's physical recovery, he was frequently in and out of Monash Hospital's Psychiatric Unit, known as P Block, often for as long as 12 months at a time. He would go in for a short stay of a few weeks because he was psychotic, but P Block was not designed to be anything but a short-term facility. Q occasionally admitted himself later, however early on in his illness most of the admissions were extremely distressing as he lacked any insight into his mental state and needed to be certified by a psychiatrist as not able to make decisions about his own welfare. That is, his rights were taken away. P Block was a locked ward, and once inside he was not allowed out. When he went in, the first thing the doctors did was to increase his medication substantially. This would immediately blunt his affect, and he wheeled around like a zombie again, his psychosis usually reduced, although it never left him. The doctors played around with the medication, experimenting with dosage levels until they felt they had it just right or as good as it was going to be. The hospital was always keen to move Q out and back home, because there would be someone else who needed a bed. Despite this, the reason Q was usually in P Block for so long was because he never seemed to improve. He usually failed to reach a point where the doctors could confidently say "Yes, Q has improved, and he is ready to re-enter society and live in the outside world." Mum, Yvette and I got very used to going to P Block for nearly 30 years. We got to know the staff, who were always caring and doing their best. Many of them truly liked Q and some of them had, as Mum would say, a bit of a soft spot for him. Even when he was unwell, he still had the ability to make people like him. It was a little bit of the old cheeky, quirky kid lurking behind his illness.

I remember once I rang Yvette when she was at Maroondah Hospital psychiatric ward to visit Q. They didn't have any beds at Monash P Block, which had become his second home and his first choice when he needed to go into hospital, although getting a bed when he needed one was always difficult. Yvette said to me "Oh my God, Q has escaped from hospital." She had driven all the way out to Maroondah, which would have been an hour each way, and they didn't say anything when she arrived. She had her young son Tim in a pram, and they were told that Q was in his bedroom, which was just around the corner. When they looked in his room it was clear he was not there, and the staff didn't know where he was. It was designed to be a locked ward like P Block at Monash, but apparently a staff member had let him go to the hospital cafeteria on his own.

Q was very persuasive and could be quite clever at manipulating people when he had a goal in mind - to escape for instance. He has since used this strategy successfully many times. Shortly afterwards they found out that a poor little old lady had rung the police and said "someone is up on my roof." Q, without legs, had climbed up a tree and made his way across and onto a random lady's house. The police quickly drove around to this very anxious lady's home and found him on the roof as she had described, delusional and with a psychotic look in his eye. At times like this, it was like he was not there, as if someone else had taken over his mind and body. Somehow the police managed to get him down and into their car, and they drove him back to Maroondah Hospital. I assume this was simply the closest psychiatric hospital rather than their knowing he had just escaped from there, but I'm not certain. When the police arrived at the hospital car park, coincidentally Yvette was out the front getting into her car with Tim. At that stage she didn't know what had happened to Q and was leaving. Q got out of the police car and into his wheelchair. He still wanted to escape - he had not yet accepted defeat and was amazingly determined. He saw Yvette and realised she was getting in her car, which presented him with another opportunity to outwit the authorities as he used to call them. With incredible speed, he wheeled over to Yvette's car, but as he tried to get into it, he ignored the car parked next to her. He opened Yvette's car door and bashed into it, but this all happened so fast that nobody had time to react. I'm not religious at all, but as Mum said, it was like he had the devil in him. Eventually the police were able to overpower him and take him back to the psychiatric ward, but at this stage Yvette was in hysterical tears seeing her brother in such a crazed state. After episodes like this, Yvette and I would usually spend a lot of time just crying as we hugged and held onto each other. It was exhausting, and very painful to watch, and it never got any easier to handle.

On one occasion, Yvette visited Q when she was pregnant with her second child, Jess. Q was in a particularly psychotic and delusional state, so they had put him in a room which they could lock. It was a padded room with nothing in it except a padded bed covered in vinyl, designed to ensure that psychotic patients had nothing they could use to harm themselves. This room was only used when patients showed extreme behaviours and simply needed time out and a period for the medication to kick in. The nurses refused to give Q his wheelchair because it was too dangerous as he could use it as a weapon. One let Yvette go into the room, and she seemed to be able to calm Q down, so when Q asked if he could go out into the courtyard for a cigarette, the nurse agreed. He crawled out on his hands and knees. He often did this, although it looked, and no doubt felt, degrading. He enjoyed his cigarette. It was dinner time, which was usually around 5pm in hospital, and so they brought him his meal. He was a passionate vegetarian by now, believing meat to be against some part of the bible, and devoured the food, including a large chicken drumstick, like an animal or a caveman.

Shortly after this he crawled back into his padded room with Yvette walking beside him. Then, without any provocation, he flew into a rage and grabbed Yvette's bag and threw it across the room, yelling obscenities at her. She was scared, especially that he might punch her in the stomach while she was pregnant with Jess and picked up her bag and ran outside. By now the staff had heard the yelling and run back to help resolve the situation, which mostly involved simply locking the door to the room and waiting until he calmed down. At times they needed more than this though, and several staff members would have to hold him down so a doctor could inject him with a sedative and antipsychotic medication.

Yvette recalls another occasion when she was visiting him at P Block and had the children with her. They were young, not yet at school, and went everywhere with her. A staff member, probably a psychiatric nurse, came up to her and said "What are you doing here with young kids? It's not safe; there are violent people in here." She went on to explain that there was one particularly violent patient, and Yvette asked why the patient was not locked in the padded room, because he might be violent with Q. Most of the time you were safe going to P Block, but you rarely saw young children in there. I always felt safe, although in the early days I was certainly uncomfortable until I got used to the environment, which was sad and depressing rather than scary or violent as many patients were shuffling around or sitting or lying down.

Yvette and I usually shared the challenges of responding when there was an emergency, though I've got to admit that Yvette probably took the lion's share of the load. A few years after those incidents, when Yvette had three young children at home, she had a call from Q late at night. He was exceedingly agitated and frightened, and said "I'm not going to survive; they're going to get me..." For him his delusions were real. There was no doubt in his mind. He was scared out of his wits. Yvette, who at this stage had separated from her husband Glenn, left her three children in bed in the middle of the night and drove 20 minutes to Q's home to help him. She took him to Monash Hospital and spent three hours in the emergency room waiting to be seen, and trying to keep Q calm so he didn't scare the other patients. They were eventually seen by a psychiatric nurse, and Yvette asked if Q could be admitted. The nurse only spent five minutes assessing Q before refusing, so Yvette had no choice but to take him back home with her. He remained very disturbed, and Yvette could not calm him down, so she lay him down to sleep on the couch in the living room. However, in his restless, anxious state he couldn't sleep, and got in his wheelchair and tried to wheel himself along the narrow hallway to the kids' rooms. He fell out of the wheelchair and onto his stumps, which began to bleed profusely, and then crawled towards the bedrooms, leaving a trail of blood. Yvette could not sleep and got up when she heard him crawling along. He said "I'm worried they're going to get your kids." Whoever "they" were, Q was clearly extremely concerned, not only about his own safety, but for the children. Yvette was petrified, and frightened that he might hurt the children. She was supposed to be at work the next morning and, so far, had had no sleep, so she called Q's case worker who was on emergency relief duties. Luckily, they were totally understanding, and able to come and pick Q up. He was taken to Monash Hospital, where he was admitted and spent many months. For the next few days Yvette was angry that she had been put in this position by the system and the psychiatric nurse who had refused to admit him. She hated being so terrified herself, and afraid that our brother would hurt her children.

The psychiatric system

The psychiatric system is a lot better now than it was 35 years ago when we first entered this world in the late 1980s, however it still has a long way to go before it is anywhere near where it should be. In the past, many patients were institutionalised, shunned, and hidden away from "normal" society. Then in the 1990s many of the "mental asylums" were closed, and people were let out into the community. However, not enough support mechanisms had been put in place, and many ended up homeless on the streets or in emergency accommodation.

Since then, beginning in the early 2000s, there has been a recognition that there needs to be a balance between supporting people with mental illnesses to live in the community as independently as possible and to be able to move people into a hospital like Monash (P Block) when necessary. This is the aim, yet the reality is very different. One of the key challenges is getting access to a bed in P Block or any other psychiatric unit quickly. Typically, a person has an episode, which creates an emergency need, but the only place that can help is the emergency department of a hospital like Monash because P Block is full and not able to cope with anyone else.

I recall once when Yvette took Q to hospital, and I met her there. He was psychotic again and needed to be hospitalised immediately. We had called P Block and were told to bring him to emergency, where Q was admitted to the standard emergency ward with other patients with physical symptoms. Given his highly agitated state, he was put in a padded room in the emergency ward, but it was not a locked room, and we were told they were waiting for a bed in P Block to become available. Q began wheeling up to patients who were physically unwell or in pain and waiting for treatment. He had physical problems at this point too - issues with his bladder due to hepatitis C. Yvette asked the doctors to give him a strong sedative to calm him down, but they refused and said they wanted to do a blood test first to help them work out what was happening with his bladder. Yvette said "You won't be able to do that, because he thinks you're trying to kill him by giving him a lethal injection," but they didn't really understand this complex psychological challenge.

The emergency ward of a hospital is extremely busy. Doctors and nurses come and go. They respond to the most urgent cases, and the ones they consider the greatest emergencies. We should have known and understood this and used it to our advantage, but we didn't. Yvette and I got him back into the padded room and tried to calm him down. We talked to him gently and tried to get him to breathe slowly and relax. I had previously done a lot of relaxation work with him, and he liked it. As I moved closer to him to continue to calm him down, totally out of the blue he punched me hard in my throat. I grabbed his hands to stop him from hitting me again, and gradually Yvette and I were able to soothe him. By this time, it was the middle of the night, and Yvette and I were exhausted. We kept him calm for eight hours throughout the night, waiting for someone to give him a sedative and/or admit him to the Psychiatric Ward. Neither of these things happened.

The police brought another very unwell psychiatric patient into the emergency ward at this point. Clearly, he had done something to warrant their involvement, and the doctors decided to move Q out of the padded room to let the new more severely affected patient have it. Q was given a normal emergency bed, while the police stood outside the padded room to ensure the other patient did not harm himself or anyone else. The next morning, Yvette left the hospital to call Mum to talk about Q's dog Charlie and make sure we asked someone to look after him, and I was left with Q. I can't quite recall exactly what happened next and why I wasn't with him the entire time, but I may have fallen asleep given we had not slept all night. All I remember is that when I looked Q was not in his bed. I must have turned around for a short while, and I was totally exhausted from hours of trying to keep him calm. I ran through the ward but couldn't find Q, so I rushed outside and saw him about 100 metres away, wheeling as fast as he could towards the main road. I sprinted past Yvette and shouted to her to get help because Q had escaped and was heading for Clayton Road. Yvette dashed inside and began shouting for help. The security guards responded instantly and came out as I hurried to the main road, where they joined me. Q was sitting in the middle of a very dangerous section of the road, but the security guards and I managed to avoid the traffic, get over to him, and make our way safely back to the emergency ward, where he was sedated immediately, and eventually taken to P Block.

After they had sedated him, Q lay in bed looking as peaceful as a sleeping baby. Yvette and I turned and hugged each other, and we both began to sob uncontrollably. He had to escape and nearly die before they would listen to us and sedate him. To be admitted into P Block, a patient with a mental illness needs to be in a terrible state. However, it was so painful to see Q like this, and the more we tried to help, the slower the doctors were in admitting him. With hindsight, we would have been better off letting him become completely agitated and cause all sorts of problems in the emergency ward. Then they would have given him the sedation he needed hours earlier. But of course, this was nearly impossible when we could see our brother in such mental pain and anguish. We went out for pizza together after this, and we both made a conscious decision that next time we would not spend hours at the hospital waiting for them to sedate or admit him; we would somehow ensure they saw him in his highly disturbed and distressed state. How shocking is it to think this was the choice we had to make? The system needs to be improved.

Wheelchair Tennis

It is incredible to think that while all this was happening, at times Q was still able to focus enough to learn to play wheelchair tennis. I was coaching tennis at Elwood Park Tennis Club from 1993 to 1997, and a few months after he left Caulfield Rehabilitation Hospital, which was about 12 months after his "accident", Q was well enough mentally to get on the tennis court again with me. We learnt together. At first Q would sit still in his old, heavy, cumbersome wheelchair and I would feed balls to him. He would enjoy hitting them back to me, and we rallied as long as we could while I hit the ball exactly where his racquet was without him having to move at all. I could see that Q loved it, and it gave him a sense of hope and the possibility of a purpose in life.

We managed to organise another wheelchair for him that was designed for sport. It was lighter, lower, and more manoeuvrable, allowing Q to learn to move around the court and to hit the ball moving. We practiced serves, volleys, smashes, and all the shots that he had been so proficient at, and we began doing some tennis drills. After some time, Q got a second wheelchair, and I learnt to play in the wheelchair too. Initially I coached him standing up, and then at the end of the session I sat in his second chair and we played a competitive game. He was much better than I was at moving around the court, since by then he had been in the chair for quite a while and the chair had become a part of him, whereas it was foreign to me. It was also quite difficult to learn to hold the tennis racquet in one hand and push yourself around with two hands, one holding the racquet. Sometimes getting a good grip on the push rim or hand rim, the part of the wheelchair next to the wheel that

Q – early days of wheelchair tennis

you use to move around, was very challenging, but I was able to play well enough to give him a reasonable game.

Once Q was playing at a reasonable level, Mum and I took him to the National Tennis Centre at Melbourne Park where he joined a wheelchair tennis squad. He started training a few times a week, and the people there were warm, friendly, and welcoming. They seemed to accept Q's sometimes strange behaviours, which was exactly what he needed. While none of them had a mental illness like Q, they were understanding and compassionate. This was where he met a wonderful young man in a wheelchair called Matt Long. Like many of the other wheelchair tennis players, Matt had been in an accident. He had a severe spinal injury but could walk a little bit although it was excruciatingly painful. In his late teens he had stopped to help a broken-down car and been hit by a passing car. Matt had used tennis to build a sense of purpose in his life too, and he and Q got on well immediately. Matt seemed to understand and appreciate Q and was very patient with him. They decided to play some doubles tournaments together. Matt was a better wheelchair singles player than Q, but Q held his own in doubles. Matt moved around the tennis court better than Q, however Q hit the ball better. His old skill had not left him, and he had lovely touch and feel of the ball.

Pretty soon, Q and Matt started winning wheelchair tennis tournaments. They peaked in the summer of 1998/9, when they won the Victorian Hardcourt Satellite tournament together and then went on to win the New South Wales Open. Their winning streak culminated with the Australian Open wheelchair doubles in January 1999, which was amazing. Q had a grand slam title to his name! It is phenomenal to consider this given what he had been through and was a testament to his determination and perseverance.

In 2000 he continued to play wheelchair tennis, and together he and Matt won the Victorian Hardcourt Satellite tournament for the second year in a row. However, as Q started to get more serious about his tennis again, I could see the pressure mounting, and he showed increasing signs of stress, anxiety, and agitation. His behaviour became more erratic, and I felt sorry for Matt, who was so generous and kind to him. Eventually they stopped playing doubles together because Q had become too unreliable. Over time Q stopped playing wheelchair tennis, which was very sad and distressing, because it was the one thing that had given him genuine pleasure and his life some purpose and meaning.

Meaning, purpose and empathy

I have thought about Q playing wheelchair tennis. We all need a sense of meaning and purpose to lead a happy and fulfilling life. Tennis gave that to Q, and for a while he was more mentally stable and engaged. Many studies have shown that meaning and purpose drive behaviour, shape choices, fuel passion, and build resilience, providing direction, focus, motivation, and a sense of fulfillment. Unfortunately, as the pressure became too much for Q, his anxiety about winning and performing reduced this pleasure, ultimately leading to his illness taking over and preventing him from playing. However, while he was playing tennis, he certainly had a more fulfilling life.

Another thing that stands out for me is the level of understanding, empathy, and compassion most of the other people in wheelchairs showed Q. It made me wonder if we need to have a traumatic experience to feel and show compassion. In this case, the other wheelchair tennis players had not had Q's experience with mental illness, but their physical disabilities transferred their empathy for physical disability to mental disability. Empathy is all about understanding another person's feelings, thoughts, and behaviour from their point of view, like being able to put yourself in their shoes - although not literally because Q no longer wore shoes. Empathy and sympathy are different. Sympathy is feeling for someone else, which tends to lead to offering advice and solutions from your own perspective, so without intending to hurt the other person, you may be pitying or patronising, leading to more discomfort for both parties. Sympathy is usually linked to a feeling of superiority, which I never felt with the wheelchair tennis players, who accepted Q as an equal and seemed to understand him. They didn't give advice or solutions: they just understood him, and displayed total empathy for him, so he felt completely comfortable with them.

Israel

Over the years, Q became increasingly religious. He became a devout Christian and believed in the Bible and all the key messages in it. He expressed a strong desire to travel to Israel and wanted to see Jerusalem - the Holy Land where Jesus' life and death unfolded. The Bible mentions Jerusalem more than any other place, and Psalm 132:13-14 states "the Lord has chosen Jerusalem and will dwell there forever". Clearly Q had read this and other passages in the Bible that demonstrated the importance of Israel and Jerusalem to people of the Christian faith. As his illness progressed, and particularly during his more psychotic phases, he spoke about going to Israel so frequently and with such passion that we had to reduce the chances that he would get on a plane and fly there. We knew that despite his determination, he would not be able to cope unless it was carefully planned, and someone who could handle him went along, so we hid his passport, and managed his bank account so that he didn't have enough money to pay for a trip. We thought this would be enough, but Q was single-minded and could achieve almost anything if he wanted it badly enough.

In 2011, Q asked Yvette to look after his dog Charlie. He said he needed a few days' break. Yvette was immediately suspicious, and she looked at him sternly and said, "Promise me you won't take off anywhere!" Q had done that many times, but he looked at her innocently and said "No, no, no, I wouldn't do that to you." Reluctantly she took Charlie, and hoped Q wouldn't leave without telling us. She also thought we were safe because we had his passport and most of his money, so if he did take off somewhere it was only likely to be a short local trip.

The next day Yvette was lying down at the Blood Bank donating blood when Q called her. She asked where he was, and Q replied, "I'm in Israel." She paused, tried to absorb this unlikely news, not quite comprehending how it could even be possible, and said "No, you're not." To which he responded, "Yes, I am, how good is it that my mobile phone works all the way over here in Israel!" It suddenly dawned on Yvette that Q was telling the truth. Somehow, he had made it to Israel. She really started to worry when he said "I'm on a bus heading towards Jerusalem, but I don't know where to stay. Can you help me find somewhere to stay?"

As soon as Yvette rang off, she called me, and asked "Hayden, are you sitting down?" I guessed something had happened to Q even before she said, "Q is in Israel!" After I had picked myself up off the floor, we began talking it all through. We couldn't understand how he had managed to get there. Later we learnt that he had gone to the Australian Passport Office in Melbourne and told them he had lost his passport, so they cancelled his old passport which we had taken and issued him with a new one. He managed to withdraw $40,000 from a bank account that he was not supposed to be able to access on his own and took the cash with him. We subsequently complained to the bank, because we had specifically arranged his account so that he could not do that. Incredibly, he just carried the money in his bum bag. He had gone to a local travel agent, and they arranged the flights for him. He had paid in cash.

Yvette and I spent the next two weeks on the phone to the Australian Embassy in Israel and the Department of Foreign Affairs, trying to find a way to get him home safely. We were desperately worried that if he became psychotic, he could end up in a psychiatric hospital or, worse, in prison, and we wouldn't be able to find him. We knew he wouldn't survive that. Furthermore, while hostilities between Israel and the Palestinians were not serious at the time, Q might not understand the need to be careful or be aware of the boundaries he needed to observe, particularly around the Gaza Strip. Although the Australian Embassy and the Department of Foreign Affairs were somewhat helpful and certainly very understanding, they couldn't do anything to bring him home or about his safety. They accepted that he had a mental illness, but said since he was an adult in Israel legally that we couldn't do anything. Q always said, "I'm an adult and I have rights, you know," an argument it was difficult to refute because I wanted him to have the right to make his own choices and decisions - but I also knew that he was not always able to make intelligent decisions in his own best interest.

Yvette ended up speaking to an Israeli taxi driver named Joseph. His English was not great, but they did manage to communicate. Q had paid Joseph to drive him around for three days, and Joseph demonstrated to us how kind, caring, and compassionate some human beings are. He could have taken advantage of Q, but he didn't. Q's clothes were filthy, so he had them washed and dried. Q also smelled bad and was dirty, so Joseph arranged for him to have a shower and clean himself up.

Joseph took Q to the Red Sea, a four-hour drive. Q desperately wanted to go swimming in the Red Sea, which he felt was holy water and had special qualities. Perhaps he believed his legs would grow back if he swam in the Red Sea. Exodus 14: 10-21 says "When the Israelites were blocked in by the Red Sea and the attacking Egyptians, God parted the Red Sea. All the people of Israel, along with their livestock, were able to cross on dry land with towering walls of water on both sides as Moses led them." When Joseph and Q arrived, they realised that Q couldn't get to the water because he was in his wheelchair and the way to the water was extremely rocky, so Joseph carried Q over the rocks and helped him into the water. Q was not a small man. He was overweight and would have been incredibly heavy to carry any distance on flat land, let alone over rocks. This showed Joseph's great humanity. We never met him but are forever in his debt.

We don't know how much of his $40,000 he ended up giving to Joseph, but I'm reasonably confident he paid Joseph well for all his help over three days, and unquestionably Joseph deserved every cent. They travelled all over Israel, which I'm pleased Q got to do, however his mental health deteriorated quite quickly, and he spent his last few days in Israel in his hotel room. The staff were delightful. We spoke with them regularly, and they were very understanding and kind to Q. They washed his clothes and brought food to his room. Yvette asked him if he was taking his medication. He had a history of not doing that when he travelled, and of course this increased his chances of becoming psychotic. He responded, "Don't worry, Bettie, I'm self-medicating with Heineken!" He could be so funny sometimes. You had to laugh even though you knew it was getting serious, and each day brought more signs that he was getting worse and becoming delusional.

Eventually we decided that I would fly over to meet him in Bangkok and bring him back safely. Yvette and I had been in continual contact with the Department of Foreign Affairs, and they managed to book him on a plane home to Melbourne, but there was a ten-hour layover in Bangkok, and we knew it would be dangerous for Q to be at the airport by himself. He could get into all sorts of trouble. He was smoking 60 cigarettes a day at this stage and would have struggled to fly from Jerusalem to Bangkok without one. He would have been craving a cigarette when he arrived in Bangkok, and immediately lit up without thinking or understanding that you are not allowed to do that. He might also be freaked out by burly security guards walking around with large guns, and we were worried that if he left the airport, we might lose him in Bangkok!

Given this, I flew over to pick him up, even though I had to suddenly abandon my work commitments and my own family. I managed to get a flight that landed an hour or two before Q was scheduled to land. I arrived on time and made my way to where Q was meant to arrive from Israel. Bangkok airport is vast, and it took some time to find the correct location. I waited nervously for an hour or more, listening out for any updates on when the plane would arrive. Finally, it landed, and people started getting off. I watched as they walked past me, becoming more despondent and worried as almost everyone disembarked, and I hadn't seen Q. I was concerned that he might not have boarded in Israel. Something might have happened at the last minute. Q might have been so psychotic that they decided he was not fit to travel alone. All these thoughts were racing through my mind as the entire plane emptied without any sign of Q. I waited and waited. The last person got off the plane, and there was still no sign of Q. I was about 40 metres or so from the door of the plane, but when I was about to give up hope, I saw Q. He was in a wheelchair being pushed by an air hostess. His normal wheelchair hadn't fitted on the plane, and he had had to wait until everyone else got off before they could help him into a narrow wheelchair that could get down the aisle, and then they transferred him to his chair. This all took time. He was looking down and hadn't noticed me. I started walking towards him as he came closer. We were about 20 metres apart when he looked up and saw me, and his eyes lit up like a little boy's. He smiled and exclaimed excitedly "Wow, it's a miracle! Hayden, you're incredible - you're a saviour. I don't know how you did it, but you have come to save me; you must be Jesus." He was clearly very happy, and yet delusional. We hugged each other for a long time, and I was immensely relieved.

The danger was far from over though. I had to take care of him for ten hours, and he was very delusional, psychotic, and anxious, and wanted a cigarette immediately as I had predicted. There were small, enclosed areas where people were allowed to smoke, so we found one of those and Q was able to satisfy his addiction, which seemed to calm him down a little bit. I had booked a hotel room at the airport as I assumed he would not be able to leave, so we made our way there, and once inside I felt safe. We had a shower and made ourselves comfortable, sat on the bed and talked, and he told me all about his travels around Israel. He was very manic. He smoked in the room, and I even had a few puffs of his cigarette to bond with him, although I wasn't a smoker and hadn't had a cigarette since I was 18 years old. He told me how the woman next to him on the plane had rats crawling all over her, and he had been tormented by them. I had visited his doctors before leaving and had his medication with me, which I gave him. It helped to calm him down a little bit, although I'm not sure if the hallucinations and delusions diminished. Perhaps they were less strong in his mind. After what seemed like an eternity keeping Q engaged and safe, we managed to get on the plane back to Melbourne. He was still anxious and delusional but calm enough to stay in his seat and not disturb the other passengers.

When we landed in Melbourne, I took Q to Mum's house, and Yvette was there. As soon as she saw Q, she went up to him and said "Q, I don't know whether to hug you or slap you!" And he smiled in his own cheeky way and immediately responded "Look at what I got you, Bettie." He had bought her a gorgeous diamond ring to thank her for everything she had done to ensure he got home safely. She was truly appreciative for this gift, but thought of me, given that I had gone all the way to Bangkok to bring him home safely, and asked "What did you get Hayden?" and Q said "Nothing." I hadn't expected anything. We took him to Monash Hospital the next day, where he spent many months again. He eventually bought me some cufflinks to thank me.

This entire Israel story is such a massive part of my memories of Q. It was always so difficult to reconcile in my mind - on the one hand, he was not leading a happy life, and he didn't have many goals or ambitions. Going to Israel was something that he wanted to do badly, and it gave him a sense of purpose and meaning. I wanted him to be happy and to have some drive in his life to provide him with a sense of fulfillment, and yet I knew that he couldn't manage it alone. The family talked about who could chaperone him, and if we could pay someone to go with him, but who had the time, energy, and skill to manage Q? We discussed the possibility of his stepbrother Kieran going. Kieran could have done it, but the timing was never quite right. We couldn't think of anyone else, because Q was so difficult to look after. He was desperately obstinate and difficult to manage, and if he had become psychotic in Israel, what would they do? In the end the only person who could possibly have managed was me, but I had a young family myself and had started a new business. Life was full. When would I find the time to go away with him for a few weeks - particularly when he spoke of going to Israel for a few months? Although I was torn, I had decided that I could not take him for the time being - perhaps later when my life was a little easier and the kids were older. They were four, seven, and nine years old. At times I felt guilty about it, however I was mostly OK with my decision, although this dual responsibility often preyed on my mind. How much time could I give to Q, my brother who needed my help and my time, and how much time did my own immediate family need? How much time did my new business need? How much time did I need to myself, to take care of my own wellbeing? There is never an easy or right answer.

Mental illness and human rights

The Israel issue made me consider human rights - that is, whenever Q became psychotic, he was unable to make decisions for himself. Later, when he realised that he was less well mentally he went to Monash P Block voluntarily, but most of his hospital admissions were involuntary. That is, he was certified by a doctor as being unable to take care of himself, and his right to make decisions about himself was taken away. He was put on a compulsory treatment order, necessary to ensure he was safe and would not harm other people.

He repeatedly ended up in hospital for many months, but he had the right to appeal this and sometimes he did. To do so Q needed to talk to his treatment team at Monash Hospital and ask for a second opinion from another psychiatrist. He had to ask why the decision had been made, seek legal advice, and then appeal the decision to hold him against his wishes at the Mental Health Tribunal. Usually, Q was not well enough or skilled enough to go through such a convoluted and complex process, and when he did manage to get a hearing at the Mental Health Tribunal, he always lost his appeal as it was clear he was not well enough to go back out into the community. In fact, it meant he was locked up indefinitely without having committed any crime.

People with mental health difficulties are over-represented in the justice system in Australia and elsewhere, and more than twice as likely to experience legal problems. A 2012 Legal Australia-Wide survey found the justice system particularly challenging for people with a mental illness. The Victorian Legal Aid organisation states clearly on their website:

> "We support all Victorians being able to live their lives with *choice and control*, having their disability appropriately taken into account at every state of the criminal justice process."

And goes on to say:

> "We recommend empowering human rights commissions to enforce anti-discrimination laws, and stronger laws imposing clear obligation on employers and education to take proactive steps to prevent discrimination, violence, abuse, neglect and exploitation."

Q was never well enough to participate in the workforce, but although I was depressed by this reality, I never observed him being exploited or abused in P Block, where the carers were always kind to him. However, the issue of choice was one I reflected on regularly. Q's rights were taken away, and he didn't have the choices I had in life. The only times when he was not treated well though were in the early days of his illness, back in the late 1980s and early '90s, when it was always the police who turned up when Q was psychotic. They were not trained in how to deal with psychosis, and only knew how to stop him physically.

Fortunately, the system has evolved and improved a great deal since then, and over the last 20 years whenever he had an episode ambulance officers came out instead of police. They were trained, and skilful at managing the myriads of scenarios and degrees of mental illness they were confronted with. While we will never eradicate mental illness, hopefully as a society we will continue to improve how we respond, provide resources and training for first responders, and learn how to show more compassion, kindness, and understanding, ensuring the physical safety of those we care about.

Delusions and Hallucinations

Q had many delusions that lasted for years once they started. As hard as we tried, we could never convince him that they were not real. He had two friends, Edward and Yusef (or Joseph as he sometimes referred to him), whom I thought were real people for a couple of years, until I realised, they didn't exist. He spoke about them as if they were real friends of his and called Monash Hospital many times looking for them. He didn't know their surnames and so the hospital staff were not able to locate them. He would call Yvette and ask "Can you help me find my friends Edward and Yusef?" They were lifelong friends whom he cared about deeply, but they didn't really exist. In fact, shortly before he died Q wrote his own eulogy and referred to Edward and Joseph in his final message to the world. He wrote "My tennis player friends, I hope to see in the future, including Edward Moses (whom I met at the Malvern Clinic) and Joseph (whom I played tennis with)." Not only did he think they were real, but in his mind, he was able to say where and when he had met them. We couldn't talk to Q about being delusional or hearing voices, because to him they were not voices. They were as real to him as real people are to you or me. Q played a tennis tournament at Nowra, an hour and a half south of Sydney, once and claimed "people from Nowra" tormented him for years afterwards.

Q lived in a one-bedroom unit in Clayton for about 27 years. It was heavily subsidised by the Victorian government, and it suited him perfectly, but two men lived at the back of his unit who also had mental illnesses, Steve and Malcolm. Q accused them both of murdering women and children and had terrible hallucinations of them chopping up bodies and putting them in rubbish bins. He was so sure of this that he called the police regularly, and on one occasion the police responded and searched Malcolm's home. Steve and Malcolm had never done anything to hurt Q, and we felt very sorry for them, because of course they hadn't done anything wrong and they themselves were suffering. In the end, Steve and Malcolm had to put up a big security fence and gate to stop Q from coming and knocking on their door and accusing them of killing people. One night Yvette had to take Q to hospital because people outside were trying to kill him.

For years, he had another imaginary friend, Isabella. One day she died, and Q was terribly upset even though she was not real. He was grieving for her like any of us would mourn the loss of a good friend.

He also had a good real friend, Tim Edwards, who was probably more delusional than he was, but who could not look after himself physically and died in his forties. They spent a lot of time together, and Tim stayed at Q's place regularly. When Yvette picked Q up to go to Tim's funeral, he said "We don't need to go to the funeral now because Tim has been resurrected. He is alive; they have cancelled the funeral." Yvette attended the funeral, which clearly had not been cancelled, and when she came back and told Q about it, he responded "My people must have got it wrong because they said he was resurrected." Q spoke about "his people". He was habitually doing what he called "his work", and he was regularly "saving them". He believed he had telepathic skills, and this was how he saved people. On one hand it was sad and upsetting for us to hear him talk in such delusional ways, and yet on the other, in a strange kind of way, we also understood that this gave him a sense of purpose. Even though he wasn't helping anyone, he felt that he was and that was enough.

In the early years, Q frequently took off without telling us. He went to Mansfield in Victoria, and Perth, Queensland, and we were desperately worried about him every time. This was before mobile phones, and we used bank records to track him as we could see where he had withdrawn money. We listed him with the police as a missing person many times, but eventually he would come home as if nothing had happened.

Later, we would plan short holidays for him. Q's favourite getaway was Airlie Beach in Queensland, where he went from time to time. We worked with his case managers and arranged for him to have enough medication to last the two weeks he would be away, and he would check in with a doctor there. The doctor would call the Mobile Support and Treatment Team, who knew Q well, and clarify the dosage of his medication because it was so high he couldn't quite believe it. But Q's delusions travelled with him wherever he went, although the change of scenery was good for him. Sometimes he went for a swim in the pool at the caravan park where he stayed, but rarely would he venture out, preferring to sit on his balcony and smoke cigarettes for most of the day. I suspect the idea of being away at Airlie Beach was better than the ultimate reality of it, but it did give him some respite for a couple of weeks, and generally he was safe in this environment.

The mental health system

I often think about the mental health system that operates in Australia, and in Victoria where we live. It is a system that has many flaws, and I have frequently been frustrated and at times angry with it. In fact, in writing this book I see that I have been more traumatised by it than I previously realised. However, it has certainly improved a great deal, and we have come a long way over the last 35 years. Furthermore, it is probably one of the best in the world as many countries show far less concern for people with mental health issues. To understand the system, its faults, its strengths, and how it has changed I will share a few stories.

As you now know, Q attempted to take his own life and, in the process, lost his legs. What you don't know is that he was compensated for this by the Transport Accident Commission. In Victoria, everyone with a driver's licence and a car pays an annual registration for the privilege of driving on our roads. A proportion of this (currently about $80 per person per year) goes to pay for an insurance scheme, the Transport Accident Act 1986, set up by the Victorian Parliament with the support of both major parties, which enabled the Transport Accident Commission (TAC) from 1 January 1987. This no-fault scheme means anyone who has an accident on the Victorian transport system, including railways, is entitled to a claim for damages, regardless of whether it was their fault or not. In a strange twist of fate that ultimately benefitted Q as he was paid a large lump sum by the TAC, which allowed him to live more comfortably than he otherwise could have on the Disability Support Pension alone. This paid for his wheelchairs, prosthetic legs, physiotherapy, and minor home alterations. It was not enough for him to buy a home for himself or lead a lavish life, but given it was his fault, I think it is an extremely generous system.

When Q spent nine months at Alfred Hospital and then had six-months of rehabilitation at Caulfield Hospital, he did not have to pay a cent for any of this world-class treatment. Most treatments in Australia's public hospitals are free for all Australian citizens and permanent residents, mainly paid for by our Medicare system. A Medicare levy of 2% of taxable income is paid by all Australians who earn enough to pay tax, currently anyone earning over $29,033 a year. The Australian Federal Government funds Australia's public hospitals jointly, and they are owned and operated by state and territory governments. It is an amazing system, and I am very happy we live in a country that values our health enough to have set up a structure whereby everyone is looked after regardless of how much money they have.

After Q's attempted suicide, he spent time at the Alfred Hospital, then at Caulfield Hospital, and then he lived at the Community Care Unit in Clayton for a further six months. In Victoria, Community Care Units or CCUs are set up by the Victorian Government to provide clinical care and rehabilitation services in a home-like environment. They support the recovery of people seriously impacted by mental illness in a community-based residential facility. The CCU was a lovely place, and it allowed Q to slowly transition out into the community safely. It fosters integration into the broader community and provides access to 24-hour multidisciplinary clinical support and treatment. Although this was not a long-term option for Q, he benefitted greatly from the accommodation and support at a critical period in his life. He had a couple of short stints in different accommodations until he became eligible for a one-bedroom unit in Clayton, part of the Victorian Government's supported accommodation scheme, where he lived for 27 years. He certainly would not have been able to afford this without government support.

Another service that was useful was the Mobile Support and Treatment Team (MSTT). Over the years Q had two case managers, Roman and Florence, who were the epitome of kindness and compassion, looked after Q for many years, and got to know him very well. They were both wonderful at recognising when he was going downhill mentally or emotionally and would arrange for him to go to P Block at Monash Hospital or to PARCS (Prevention and Recovery Care Service), a residential facility helping for adults recovering from acute mental health issues and funded by the Department of Human Services. These facilities are staffed 24 hours a day, seven days a week. Q was on a Community Treatment Order for many years, which meant that if he didn't take his medication, he could be put straight back into P Block. Roman or Florence would visit him at home once a week to give him a slow-release injection. They would also visit another two or three times a week to watch him take his oral medication, and then give him enough for the next couple of days. This meant that if Q didn't take it at least he had only missed a day or two and still had the effects of the injection to reduce the chance of a steep decline in his mental stability.

As you can see, there are many wonderful aspects of the system that surrounds and supports people with a mental illness, however a few stories stand out in relation to continued problems. Q was in and out of Monash Psychiatric Hospital for about 27 years. The decision on who gets in and who doesn't is made by a nurse. A psychiatrist arrives a little while later to review the decision, and usually confirms it. From a safety perspective, the nurse, generally female, is in a room with the patient, who must be very mentally unstable to be there, for 40 minutes without any protection. This system is not ideal for patients or for staff making these assessments. It is exceedingly difficult for a patient to get admitted, and often a highly traumatic experience. The lack of strong protocols in the admissions process, especially staff safety, needs to be reviewed and improved.

Q regularly spent many months, at times almost 12, in hospital once he was admitted. This is far from ideal. A psychiatric hospital ward is not intended nor designed for long-term care. In fact, it is intended for a stay of only a few weeks, however Q often couldn't get out because he frequently went downhill in hospital rather than improving. P Block did offer activities such as art classes, but they were of little value if Q was too unwell to take them. Furthermore, he never had any form of talking therapy. When it was offered, he didn't seem to want to talk, but it was not offered at P Block. As a cognitive behavioural psychologist, I have been frustrated for years by this fault in our system. The research and the evidence are clear: several different talking therapies such as Cognitive Behavioural Therapy (CBT), have been shown to produce positive results.

The COVID-19 pandemic was clearly a challenging time for many people. For a two-year period during the many lockdowns in Melbourne, Q and I spoke to each other daily on the phone. When the lockdowns began, he was anxious, so I asked him if he wanted to do some relaxation sessions with me. He agreed readily, so I spent 15 minutes every day with him doing what he called relaxation therapy. He looked forward to it, and so did I. I would put my AirPods on, lie down, and ask Q to do the same. When he sounded ready, I would ask Q to put the phone on speaker next to his head. Q would tell me when he had done this and was ready to begin. Initially I experimented with various relaxation techniques to see what would work best for him, and eventually we found an approach he seemed to like. I began by asking him to focus on his breathing, first simply paying attention to his breath, and then aiming to slow his breathing down. I added some visualisation next. He loved the beach and so I would take him on a journey there, and together we would watch the waves gently rolling in and out. This would be followed by a full body scan using a progressive muscular relaxation technique that Q enjoyed. It gave him somewhere to put his mind and a small window of respite. Finally, we finished with a minute of silence as we both liked the relaxed sensation. When we finished, I'd sometime ask, "How was that, Q?" and he would usually say "Wow, that was great, Hayd." He loved it, so we spent 15 minutes every day for two years doing it. He would call me up and ask, "Can we do relaxation therapy today?" I'd say "Of course, what time?" He usually had nothing on, so we worked around my schedule. I was always able to find 15 minutes, and it was good for me too, and forced me to stop and slow down.

Q was bored in hospital. That didn't help him recover, and only acerbated his mental health problems. At one point, the hospital introduced a no smoking policy. I understood that they needed to have this rule for the general hospital, but it was ridiculous for psychiatric patients because most of them, including Q, were heavy smokers. Q smoked about 60 cigarettes a day, therefore going into hospital to get better was impossible because not smoking made him very anxious, and his mental health deteriorated immediately. At times I felt like a criminal as I smuggled packets of cigarettes into P Block and gave them to Q. I used to put a few packets down my pants, and then once inside in a private place with Q, I would take them out and give them to him. He hid them somewhere on his body or in his wheelchair and found a way of having a naughty cigarette in secret places. During lockdown he was in P Block, and we couldn't go in to see him, so we arranged a very elaborate way of getting him cigarettes. We walked past a P Block wall and called Q on his mobile phone. He said "Now!" when the area was clear of staff, and we threw the packets of cigarettes over the wall, and he caught them and hid them. This was ludicrous. How can a mentally unwell patient go somewhere for help, only to be told they must give up smoking whilst going through a traumatic psychotic episode?

The mental health system was very frustrating to deal with. In 2013, there was an episode that caused Yvette and me considerable distress. On Friday, 28 June at 12:10am Yvette had received a phone call from Q, who was terrified. He thought "they" were outside his house, trying to get in to kill him. He mentioned suicide because he couldn't cope with these people who wouldn't leave him alone. Yvette called the Crisis Assessment Team, and spoke to a man who told her to either ring an ambulance or take him to hospital herself. Yvette picked Q up and drove him to Monash Medical Centre, where she waited with him in the emergency department until about 3:30am. He was delusional, and very distressed and anxious. There were a pregnant woman, a baby, and several children in the waiting room, and Yvette feared that Q might behave violently in the state he was in. Finally, they spoke to a psychiatric nurse. Q spent less than five minutes with him, while he asked a few questions. Somehow Q managed to pull himself together in front of the nurse - which he was often able to do - and responded with much more thought and consideration than his previous behaviour would have suggested possible. Yvette tried to clarify a few points, but the nurse would not listen to her at all and would not admit Q because the Mobile Treatment and Support Team were involved. He told Yvette to call Q's case manager at 8am. We found out later that his case manager had been trying to get him admitted to hospital earlier that day, but no beds were available. Yvette told the psychiatric nurse that Q had mentioned he was suicidal earlier, so the nurse asked him "You won't do anything to hurt yourself, will you?" and Q replied sensibly "Of course not. I've done that before and I'll never do that again." The nurse stood up to leave and Yvette asked "Are you serious? Is that it?" He said "Yep, that's it" and walked away.

Understandably Yvette left the hospital in tears, exhausted, drained, and terrified of having to deal with Q in this state by herself with her three children asleep at home alone. Yvette drove Q back to her house and, reluctantly, he went to bed. She made her children's school lunches at around 5am, then went to bed herself. Not long after this she heard Q get up and go down the hallway and open the kids' bedroom doors to check on them and make sure they hadn't been murdered. She tried to get him to go back to bed, but he said, "How can I fucking go to sleep when people are outside trying to get in and kill us all?" This continued for the next few hours. Yvette was too scared to go to sleep in her own home. She called me shortly after this, and I rang the case manager at 8am and was able to get the paperwork signed for him to be admitted involuntarily. The case manager picked him up at 11:30am and took him to Monash where he was finally admitted.

Yvette was furious about the way she had been treated by the psychiatric nurse, and she wrote a formal complaint to Southern Health, saying that she had gone to the hospital to ask for help for a very sick brother who clearly needed to be in hospital, that Q's state of mind had been deteriorating for several months, and that he thought people were talking telepathically to him and saying all sorts of horrible things. He was a danger to himself and to others and had needed 24-hour care immediately. The psychiatric nurse, who should have known better and been able to see what was really going on, seemed to have no understanding of mental illness and had no compassion for the situation. Q spent about two months in hospital on this occasion, proving that he absolutely needed to be admitted.

On another occasion, on 14 February 2017, Yvette sent a second official complaint. Q had been in P Block since 27 December 2016, his fourth admission in less than 12 months. He continued to have horrendous paranoid delusions that his neighbours Steve and Malcolm had been torturing and murdering women and children and chopping up their bodies, and he constantly heard them screaming. Q had harassed Steve and Malcolm for years and rung their doorbell hundreds of times. Due to this ongoing traumatic scenario, he didn't want to return to his unit in Clayton, so we had a family meeting at Monash Hospital. Also at the meeting were three psychiatrists, two psychiatric nurses, a social worker, Q's case manager, Q, Yvette, Mum, Dad, and me. We all agreed that Q couldn't return to live there and put in an application to the Ministry of Housing for a new unit. In the meantime, we agreed, Q would live at PARCS, an adult Prevention and Recovery Care community-based service providing short-term residential care in Narre Warren, for about six months. But that day Steve died of cancer, and Q laughed hysterically and said, "I can go home now!" While Steve had been the main perpetrator in Q's delusions, Malcolm sometimes was too, and Q had recently told a nurse that Malcolm had held a gun to his head. We knew this was not true, but Q believed it. He had called Yvette and me at least 12 times each the previous day and told us he was being discharged. We told him he wasn't going home; he was going to PARCS as we had all agreed at the meeting. He screamed at Yvette "I'm not going to that hellhole; I'm a grown man and you can't make me!" He wasn't normally like this, but his behaviour had become increasingly aggressive – a strong sign he was becoming increasingly mentally unstable.

Yvette called the psychiatric nurse on duty and confirmed Q was not going home and was going to PARCS. She then asked the nurse to confirm that as an involuntary patient he couldn't discharge himself. The nurse confirmed that Q was under a Community Treatment Order and therefore couldn't discharge himself from PARCS. At 10am the next morning Yvette received a message from P Block confirming the discharge plan and that Q was going to PARCS that day. At 11am, when Yvette called back and asked how Q was getting to PARCS, she was told by a nurse there was a problem, and they were trying to find a staff member to take him. He confirmed that Q was going to PARCS, and said "We agree with you, he can never return to his unit in Clayton." Yvette said "Good, because he believes Malcolm held a gun to his head, and yesterday he said that Malcolm had to pay for this."

At 3:45pm that day, Q called Yvette and said that he had been discharged and was in a taxi on his way home. Yvette immediately called the nurse's station at P Block, who confirmed this. When she asked who had made the decision, she was informed that two of the treating psychiatrists had. Yvette burst into tears of frustration and utter disbelief, appalled that after all these conversations he could simply be put in a taxi, given a cab charge voucher, and sent home. He didn't even have house keys. Yvette spoke to Q again, terrified that he might do something to Malcolm in revenge. She asked him to promise her that he would leave Malcolm alone and just let it be, but he responded, "You know what they say in the Bible, Yvette?" When she replied "No, I don't," he said "The Bible says not to make promises you can't keep." This only alarmed Yvette more, and she wrote to the hospital asking "Where is the hospital's duty of care to Q, to Malcolm, and to us his family who have to pick up the pieces every time he relapses like this?" She continued "We have unfortunately been let down too many times to mention by the public hospital system while dealing with this chronic mental illness and crying out for help from professionals. This is one more to add to the list.

I really hope Q doesn't do anything stupid to hurt himself or anyone else while he has such horrible psychotic thoughts."

Yvette received a reply a day later on 15 February 2017. While the hospital did apologise for this distressing situation, they provided an unsatisfactory explanation: that Q's treating psychiatrist had given the clinical handover of his care to the PARCS team the previous day as planned. The Mobile Support and Treatment Team (MSTT) were also given a clinical handover for his ongoing care in the community. Since he was being discharged from hospital, his treatment order was changed from involuntary patient to a Community Treatment Order, which meant that he had rights again and could legally refuse to go to PARCS, which he did. A PARCS admission can't be forced, we were now advised and must be agreed by "the consumer".

To manage the risks involved, we were told that the police had been informed, and the MSTT involved, and his case worker was going to visit him that afternoon, so they felt that they could supervise this situation in this way.

So, after all the meetings, discussions, agreements, and confirmations that he would never go home again due to the risks, he was sent home due to a legal technicality that was never considered or discussed, even though Yvette had specifically raised this potential issue with one of the psychiatric nurses and was promised it would not happen. Unfortunately, it did happen on many occasions over the 30 years that Q went in and out of hospital. We understood that the system could not cope with the demand for services and there was always a shortage of beds when you needed one, however this was inexcusable. Q was in danger of hurting himself and Malcolm, and a bed was available, but the communication and execution of the discharge plan were extremely poor and resulted in increased anxiety, distress, and real concern that something might go wrong. Luckily Q did not hurt himself or Malcolm over the coming days, weeks, or years, but we could not count on this at the time. Yvette has told me her heart sank every time she heard a story on the news about anyone psychiatrically unwell killing someone, fearing that could happen in our family. Her worst fear was that Q, in an extreme delusional state, might hurt someone. He normally wouldn't hurt a fly when he was thinking more clearly but was totally unpredictable when psychotic.

This demonstrates that the system was far from perfect, although I recognise and acknowledge that everyone was doing their best. Most of the staff truly cared about their patients, but the system often broke down with unintended consequences. People who work in the mental health system play an extremely challenging, complex, and demanding role in the lives of people like Q. There is no one simple solution to this terrible problem, however I certainly believe that a review of the mental health area from a systems and holistic perspective would be extremely helpful.

Although I consider Q unlucky to have developed schizophrenia, and myself extremely blessed not to have it, there is no question that Q was fortunate to have a family that loved and supported him throughout his 35 years of mental illness. Some people do not have family. One such person is a man named Peter. After Steve died, Peter moved into in the unit behind Q with Malcolm. Peter had no family to support him and led a very lonely life. My mother has always been a very caring woman, and she got to know Peter, and found out that he had been on the same medication for 20 years and had been seeing the same GP. Mum, who is 86 years old now, recently made some enquiries on his behalf and was able to get him accepted into a National Disability Insurance Scheme (NDIS) program. He was reassessed and is now doing much better on a different level of medication. The changes in his medication reduced the time he spent sleeping, which had been 12-14 hours a day, and the quality of his life has improved dramatically. Our mental health system relies strongly on family to do a lot of the heavy lifting, and occasionally a lovely little old lady like my mother is there to help and show kindness and compassion. Mum is also an NDIS nominee for a lady named Grace, who has no family in Australia. What will happen to these two people when Mum is no longer around?

The NDIS provides funding for eligible people with a physical or mental disability to spend more time with family and friends and have greater independence and an improved quality of life. It also connects people with a disability to services in their community, such as doctors, community groups, sporting clubs, and support groups. Over 600,000 Australians with a disability have access to the services and support they need, although the program has been widely criticised for its bureaucratic processes, cost overruns, and some shonky NDIS providers. Q benefitted greatly from this program and was able to access several services that made his life considerably better. And he had a carer, who spent three hours with him three times a week.

We were extremely lucky to find a woman called Clare, who was quite simply marvellous, and wonderful with Q. She got to know him very well, and he really liked her. She spent three or four hours with him two or three times a week and I consider Clare a family friend and not just a paid carer. Sometimes she would clean his unit up a little bit, other times she would drive him to various appointments, but the best times were when they would enjoy quality time together. They laughed together, and she was patient, kind, caring, and thoughtful. Clare got to know Q well, and when she realised that he loved to sing and especially The Doors, she bought him a microphone and a sound system. She took a video of him singing along to 'Love Her Madly', and I can still picture him singing his heart out "Don't you love her as she's walkin' out the door?"

One of the worst elements of schizophrenia is the loss of many friends and the associated loneliness, so the burden gets heavier and more intolerable for family members. Having someone like Clare to care for him a couple of times a week gave us a break, and he was being looked after and had company he enjoyed. This made a massive difference to his life, and to Mum's, Yvette's and my lives too. Q also had someone who came and cleaned his unit for him, but he really looked forward to Clare's visits and their time together. That gave him a real sense of joy. It was so good to witness these periods of happiness amid his suffering and uncertainty.

Being in a wheelchair, he was not physically able to vacuum or mop floors, change bedsheets, or clean the shower, and even though he was physically able to do many things, he was not well enough mentally. Unfortunately, many people with severe mental illness do not think about their surroundings, and personal hygiene and cleaning are the last things they consider. Q's unit was kept clean, and he also had someone who did a weekly food shop for him, which meant he only had to take care of short-term needs like milk, bread, and cigarettes. Clare and Q's cleaner both made him nice sandwiches or cooked meals for him, which meant at least he ate well on those days.

Have things improved over 35 years? Yes, absolutely they have. While we still have a long way to go, the system is a lot better than it was. NDIS has made a positive difference. The stigma in the community is far less than it was. People can talk about mental illness and mental health issues more openly now. We are improving.

Back to Craig – don't forget me

Q's life and his sad plight were always front and centre in our family. We had countless serious events and dramas to deal with over many years and were not paying enough attention to Craig and his challenges. It is clear now with hindsight that Craig felt neglected – like a little child standing there yelling "What about me?" It is strange to say that he was jealous of Q. You might wonder how anyone could be jealous of the life Q had, but it does make sense when you put yourself in Craig's shoes. He craved attention and love. He never felt Dad loved him. He was kicked out of his home when he was only 17. He felt rejected, which led to an extremely low level of self-worth, defined by Merriam-Webster as "a feeling that you are not a good person who deserves to be treated with respect."

Self-worth is at our core; it influences our thoughts, feelings, and behaviours daily, and is at the heart of how we value ourselves as human beings. The opposite of low self-worth is self-acceptance, which is frequently found through achievement, and sometimes through competition. When we do well against other people, we feel pride, which helps us to accept ourselves.

Craig struggled to achieve and compete in many areas of life. One of the outcomes of his intellectual disability was that he became frustrated because he was not able to do things other people could do, and this led to him becoming angry and getting into fights, but the anger masked severe anxiety and depression. He had been told for many years that he was lazy, and desperately needed a label to prove that it wasn't his fault. Q had a label, and everyone realised that his behaviour was not his fault, and he received love and attention, but Craig felt he was blamed for the way he behaved and didn't have the acceptance he craved. In 1999, at the age of 36, Craig was officially diagnosed with suffering from anxiety and depression. Then in 2001, he applied for and received a disability pension for having this illness. Ironically this helped him, because finally he had a label, proof it was not his fault. He had an illness that contributed to his difficulties in life, and he began to get some positive attention.

Craig badly wanted attention from women. Interestingly, he has rarely had difficulty finding women who wanted to have relationships with him - his challenge has always been either keeping them for long or finding women who are good for him. When Craig was about 37 in 2000, he was working as a taxi driver. One night he picked up a woman, Kay Seaton, who was 50 years old. Craig asked for Kay's phone number and, surprisingly, she gave it to him. They ended up going out together for a little over 13 months - Craig's longest relationship. Kay was good for Craig. She was reasonably normal, and their relationship was a healthy one. Unfortunately, Kay's brother didn't like Craig, and eventually his constant criticisms led to Kay leaving him. Craig was devasted for quite some time after this. His next longest relationship was with Gabrielle, whom he dated for over two and a half years, with a break of about nine months in the middle. This was mostly positive for Craig, although Gabrielle was much more of a roller-coaster ride than Kay.

In July 2011, Craig started dating Kathy, and this relationship totally changed the course of his life - mostly not for the better. When their relationship began, Kathy was nine weeks pregnant by a man named Donald. This was an ominous beginning, although Donald and Kathy were no longer together, and he had left for Adelaide. In 2011, Donald committed a murder for which he was later jailed - although it was reduced to a manslaughter charge - and he was released in 2020. Donald is a huge man of about 6 feet 7 inches. On 7 March 2012, Craig's stepson John was born, a healthy, normal baby. Kathy has had her challenges in life too: she has a mild intellectual disability and is on the spectrum with unconfirmed autism. My mother helped her get a disability pension.

Craig and Kathy stayed together and raised John for seven years. John is now 12, and he calls Craig Daddy. Over those first seven years they loved John very much and did the best they could to raise him however much they struggled, but Kathy could not control John and found even the most basic parenting skills too difficult. For example, if John caught a common cold, she did not know what to do so she would take him to the emergency department of the local hospital. At seven he was strong and very big, and difficult to manage physically, so when he pulled the curtains down and threw things around and broke them, Kathy hid in the toilet and called the police.

As his stepfather rather than his biological father, Craig never felt he could discipline John the way a "real" father might. When John was three or four, he would refuse to put his seat belt on in the car. Kathy would try her best to get him to, but eventually gave up. Craig would try to force John to put it on, and then Kathy would tell Craig off for using force.

Throughout these seven years, Mum, Yvette, and I did our best to help them both learn how to bring John up, but unfortunately in the end it was too much for Kathy, and in April 2019 she decided she couldn't do any more and drove him to the Department of Health and Human Service (DHHS) in Frankston to speak to them about putting John into foster care.

Shortly before this, Craig and Kathy had decided that they would separate but remain good friends, which they are to this day. They still live near each other and care for each other deeply. Craig was still helping Kathy with John, but the separation caused him awful emotional turmoil and pain.

Kathy left John with the DHHS, who could not find suitable foster care immediately and put him into a hotel. The next day, Craig attended a case in the Magistrates Court in Moorabbin, where Kathy was seeking to have John looked after by foster carers and wanted to relinquish her rights as a mother. Although Craig agreed that Kathy was not coping and it was probably best if John were adopted, he never realised this would mean he might not get to see John again. He desperately wanted to stay involved and be John's father, although he recognised, he did not have the coping skills either to do this on a full-time basis. Sharing the parenting with Kathy was best combined with each of them having some respite on their own without John. That helped them both to get along and survive, but separately neither could manage. The DHHS encouraged Kathy not to let go of her rights as a mother, and she equivocated in court, unsure of whether she was doing the right thing as she loved John dearly, as did Craig.

I attended Court on that day to support Craig and Kathy and was disappointed to find out that Craig was not a party to the case and therefore had no rights. He was not even allowed to speak in court. We asked if we could have a legal aid lawyer to represent Craig but were told that legal aid was only available for a party to a case, and while Craig had been the stepfather, he was not living with Kathy then, and so he was not given a say in what happened to John.

When John was two years old, Craig was struggling with his role as John's father. He was not the biological father, and therefore seemingly not entitled to act like the "real father". Craig's mental health issues had escalated, and he had become increasingly manic and agitated. He was never violent, but sometimes he became angry, although he did realise when he was not well mentally. He went to the psychiatric ward of the Frankston Hospital, where he was admitted and remained for four weeks, his first and last time in a psychiatric hospital. His medication was adjusted, he improved, and since then I have rarely seen Craig act in an aggressive manner. In fact, most of the time he is the exact opposite, and although he frequently becomes anxious, it rarely turns to anger. Today he is much more appreciative and grateful for any help he gets, and regularly thanks me and our sister for all the little things we do for him. He is fun and laughs easily.

John was put into foster care in April 2019 through the Treatment Foster Care Oregon (TFCO) program, a six-to-12-month program that focuses on behaviour modification and social learning theories. Attached to the program to support John were a skills coach, individual therapist, teacher, and a family therapist to support Kathy, but unfortunately Craig was not included in this family support.

While all this was playing out, John was in a foster home with several other children. We were kept up to date with his progress through Craig and Kathy and knew that he hated it. He was in the care of the DHHS but living in the foster home where he was bitten by another child, smoked a bong with a teenage boy, and was shown pornographic material on an iPad by another boy. Eventually he moved on and had a more positive experience staying with a woman called Lola.

Meanwhile, Kathy had been provided with various types of support to teach her to improve her parenting skills, and the DHHS started to think that it would be best for John to move back with her. They put a transition plan in place between September 2020 and February 2021 to ensure Kathy could cope better and allowed Craig a one-hour Facetime session with John per fortnight. Often these sessions would not happen at all or be delayed with no communication from the DHHS, and no apology nor even an attempt to reschedule them. The Facetime sessions didn't go well anyway as John had difficulty concentrating, and Craig was not very good at talking to John on Facetime.

Craig felt that his relationship with John was slipping away, and unfortunately while all the legal issues and care plans were playing out things were not improving for Kathy and John either. In January 2021, I received a text message from Craig saying "John is smashing up the house and Kathy has called the police." I immediately telephoned Craig and asked him to call Kathy and get her to ring me before calling the police as I believed I might be able to avoid the police coming to the house and give Kathy advice about what to do. Unfortunately, Kathy did not want my help and called the police, who came and spent an hour with her and John.

We are now five years on from the first time Kathy decided to take John to the DHHS and offer him up for adoption, and Craig is still only allowed to see him for an hour a week in supervised visits in a small room at the DHHS, which has now changed its name to DFFH - the Department of Family, Fairness and Housing. Craig is not able to spend any quality time with John, and he finds the environment awkward. He doesn't know how to interact with John in any meaningful way, and desperately wants to have unsupervised time with him so that they can do fun things together.

Meanwhile, John has been in and out of foster care, kinship care, and residential care. Foster care is temporary care of children by trained, assessed, and accredited foster carers when the child is not able to receive care from a relative. Kinship care is provided by relatives of a member of a child's social network when a child cannot live with their parents. Beyond foster care and relative/kinship care, there are also long-term guardianship carers where children are placed with a carer until they are 18 years old, and respite carers. Respite care is short-term placements for weekends or a few weeks.

Another option in Australia is residential care. Residential care is a placement service for children and young people in the Child Protection system. These homes are run by Community Service Organisations, and there are usually many children in each home. Children and young people who live in residential care have usually experienced the greatest level of trauma and require expert therapeutic care and support. They either display challenging behaviour or are part of a larger sibling group. The challenge is that many young people in a group home environment have been raised in a traumatic context and are frequently quite delinquent, and they influence others living in this small community, which only exacerbates the problems. John has been exposed to violence and illegal drugs in residential care, and he is only 12 years old. Out-of-home care in Australia is a response to the complex problems involved in looking after children whose parents are not able to do so. I do not have any solutions. I just know that it doesn't work well now, and the children are the ones who suffer most.

John spends unsupervised time with Kathy, and then returns to the residential care arrangement. He is suffering badly as he wants to be with Kathy, but she does not look after him well, which is a considerable risk to him, mostly because she still does not understand the need to put any boundaries around his behaviour. For years he refused to go to school, so he missed out on education and socialisation with other children. He has attended school more recently because of living with either a foster carer or in residential care, and was improving, however when he demonstrated aggressive behaviour at school he was suspended briefly.

Our family is concerned that John will be like his biological father and end up in prison. We have done everything we can to help to create an environment where he gets the education and support, he needs to be a positive and productive part of our society, but there is still a strong chance he is heading for trouble. After his poor start in life, it will be remarkable if he is able to find a constructive way through this mess.

A qualification to parent, and support for those who struggle

—

I have wondered about the power we all have as human beings to bring a child into this world, despite sometimes lacking the capacity to take care of that child. Kathy gave birth to John, and yet she has never had the skills needed to set him up for any positive kind of life. To me this is both obvious and sad, however I don't know what the solution is. Clearly none of us knows if we are going to be good parents. What is the definition of a good parent anyway? I have even wondered if we should introduce a course for new parents to teach them to be good parents. I am aware that a University of Queensland-developed program designed to improve the health and wellbeing of children and families is available in 26 countries. The aim of this program is to improve parents' emotional wellbeing and happiness by providing coping skills and strategies to help them teach their children new skills, manage behaviour, and guide development. Should programs like this be made mandatory? How else could we help improve parenting so that these tragic situations can be avoided?

In Australia, thousands of parents struggle to take care of their children for various reasons. The child protection law says that children and young people must be kept safe and healthy, and protected from harm. A child may be harmed or neglected, for example, physically, sexually or emotionally threatened or hurt, or lack food, clothing, shelter, or medical care. Or may not have proper parental supervision.

While the protection of the child is paramount, Child Protection services' philosophy is to involve and include the family as much as possible, and to seek ways to encourage the parent or parents to take better care of their child or children. Unfortunately, often the family is not able to do this, so then where do the children go? The options in our society are not good.

According to the Australian Institute of Health and Welfare, around 46,000 children are currently in out-of-home care in Australia, and there are only about 9,000 foster carer households. Over half of foster parents have several children placed with them. In addition, there are about 15,600 relative/kinship carer households.

I was asked if John could come and live with me and my family on a permanent basis. We discussed this as a family, but declined as we decided it would be too complicated and create serious problems for my own children.

Glenn – Spiralling down

My sister Yvette is four years younger than I am. She was born in 1971. She must have had a tough early life, growing up with three older brothers, two of whom had serious problems. We were all rough, and she didn't get a lot of empathy and care or love. Craig used to push and shove her around without realising his own strength, and Q used to hit her. He would chase her around the house with a feather duster, corner her in the laundry and hit her with the cane end. Somehow, she made it through her early years, became tough and resilient, and grew up to be one of the normal ones in our family. Now she is the most empathetic, caring, and compassionate person I know.

Yvette moved out at the age of 18. She met Glenn, and in 1996, a little over four years later, they were married. We all liked Glenn a lot. He was a kind, thoughtful, gentle man, quietly spoken, who always gave you his full attention. Glenn was a family man, the youngest child of Kevin and Jenny, with an older brother Gary and sister Cherryn. He worked in the family concreting business with his father, brother, and brother-in-law Viv. They became Melbourne's premier supplier of decorative exposed aggregate concrete. Glenn's father Kevin had worked there until he retired, and Glenn liked the fact that it was a family business. He felt a strong sense of duty and obligation to his family.

Yvette and Glenn had three children, Tim, Jess, and Georgia. Raising children is a crazy roller coaster and mixture of emotions for any parent, and with three children myself I know the incredible joy that kids provide. You feel so much warmth, affection and love for your children.

When they are little, they do countless things that make you smile as you watch them grow up curious about the world they live in. To see the world through a child's eyes is extremely helpful for adults as we tend to lose sight of some of its wonders. On the other hand, raising children presents many challenges and is probably one of the hardest things in life. When you have three young children, they demand all your attention most of the time. Young couples consistently struggle with this. They need to juggle many competing demands including working to pay for daily needs, finding time to be together, often the hardest thing, and coping with the constant needs of three little humans who frequently push and challenge their parents.

Over time, I began to observe that these challenges affected both their marriage and Glenn's behaviour. Working in the family business was relentless and physically demanding. Glenn would leave home around 6am or earlier, and usually worked in the yard mixing cement or drove trucks all day long. He would get home late, around 7 or 8pm, covered in dust and totally exhausted. He did this six days a week, and it began to take a toll on him personally and on his marriage to Yvette and his relationship with their children. Glenn liked a drink with his mates, and on Saturday nights he would drink quite heavily until late at night or the early hours of the morning, so he spent much of Sunday recovering from that and from his enormous workload.

While he was a strong family man in spirit, sadly this pattern meant he had little time for Yvette and the kids, and Yvette felt like a single parent. Glenn couldn't help with any parenting duties for six days of the week, because he would be gone in the morning before anyone was up and return late when the kids had gone to bed or were just going. The only day he could possibly have helped with the kids was Sunday, but he was not able to play much of a role there either because he was simply too exhausted and/or hung over. Yvette had all the responsibility for raising three children, and gradually became increasingly frustrated with Glenn and his unhealthy behaviour, and Glenn became increasingly withdrawn. In addition to this, Glenn's psychological state was slowly deteriorating, and he became depressed, quiet, and solitary. He once said that he had always felt a little bit different from other people but had never talked about it.

It was clear to anyone watching that the work environment was contributing to his problems. Glenn needed to leave the family business to have any chance of turning his life and relationships around. There was no balance in his life – inevitably, when he worked such long hours, day after day, week after week, month after month, and year after year. We talked about this for several years, however he felt torn apart, guilty because he didn't want to let the family down by leaving, and his strong sense of loyalty and obligation to them meant, ironically, that he didn't prioritise his immediate family of Yvette and the three children, who all needed him desperately.

Eventually Glenn did leave the business. He worked with a great mate of his, Bruno, and his brother Johnny as a builder, and they did lots of home renovations. Glenn worked much more reasonable hours, from 8am till 4pm, and became a different person. The old Glenn came back to life, and he had a little sparkle in his eye and was no longer down and forlorn. His mood also improved, he had time for the kids, and even his relationship with Yvette got better. Things were looking up. Unfortunately, it didn't last. After about six months his brother Gary asked him to come back to fill in for someone for a short while. Yvette begged him not to, but his sense of loyalty was too strong, and despite knowing it was not a good idea he felt compelled to help. This turned into a full-time job again, and he was back in the family business on a permanent basis. The old patterns resurfaced.

Once when Georgia was a toddler, Yvette was bathing her one evening and rang Glenn to see if he was coming home after work. It was after 8pm and he said "I'm in Mansfield (about three hours' drive away). I've gone to look at a caravan." This was erratic behaviour from Glenn. Apparently, he had left work around midday and driven all the way to Mansfield without telling anyone. Another time Yvette came home with the kids as Glenn was walking out the door with an overnight bag. She asked, "Where are you going?" and he replied, "I'm going out." She asked "Where?" and he responded, "I don't know; I'm just going." So, she said, "What will I tell the kids?" And he said, "I don't know." And left.

Glenn still smiling for the camera despite the inner turmoil

Yvette rang Glenn's mum Jenny and told her. She was worried he might take his life and checked the medicine cabinet to make sure he had not taken anything dangerous. He had been extremely depressed and was clearly in a confused state. When Yvette rang him later that night, he had driven to Lakes Entrance about three hours away and checked into a motel. He had been trying not to drink alcohol, but that night he had succumbed and drunk a full bottle of ouzo. Yvette asked, "You're not going to hurt yourself, are you?" and he replied "No." This type of behaviour was escalating, and Yvette went through many months of it, and walking home to check that he was still alive. She desperately didn't want the children to find him dead one day, and would get back from school pick-ups, footy training, or kindergarten, and ask the children to check the letter box so they were distracted, and she could run inside to make sure that he hadn't committed suicide.

When Glenn had stayed in bed for weeks, Yvette sat on the edge of the bed and said "I'm not naïve. I know how depressed you are. I know how much you're struggling. Are you thinking of ending your life?" and he replied, "If it wasn't for you and the kids, I would." Yvette said "Please promise me you'll never do that to us. Please keep fighting." Glenn didn't reply.

On one occasion, Yvette came home and found Glenn sitting on the ground out the back of their house in tears. She had never seen him cry. He then lay on the couch for six weeks, and at one point he said to Yvette "I do realise I'm cramping your style." Yvette and the children had friends coming over, and Glenn was lying on the couch unable to move. Clearly, he realised his situation but was unable to do anything about it.

Glenn had been seeing a GP who specialised in men's mental health and had been on anti-depressants for a few years. Antidepressants work on several chemicals in the brain called neurotransmitters. They are all intended to influence mood positively, but unfortunately for Glenn they didn't help his mood. They also had terrible side effects such as chronic insomnia. He sometimes felt that he had electric sparks going through his body, and had a constant dry mouth and tight jaw, which led to terrible tension headaches.

Glenn tried many different antidepressants, to no avail. Typically, you need to take antidepressant medication for at least two to four weeks to start feeling better, however it can take up to six to eight weeks to feel the full effect. For some people, antidepressants do not work, no matter how long they take them for, and Glenn was one of those. After no improvement in his mental health, he started seeing a psychiatrist, who thought that rather than having depression, Glenn had bipolar 2 disorder. Bipolar 2 is slightly different from bipolar 1. The main difference between bipolar 1 and 2 is the severity of the symptoms. People with bipolar 1 disorder experience more severe highs (mania) and may not have depressive symptoms. Whereas people with bipolar 2 experience less severe hypomania, and their diagnosis includes more severe depressive episodes. Glenn's manic phase was like most people's normal behaviour, but his depressive behaviours were extremely low. The psychiatrist experimented with several different mood stabilisers for quite a few months on each one, but none of them worked.

With very few treatment options open to the psychiatrist, he suggested electroconvulsive therapy (ECT). ECT involves a brief electrical stimulation of the brain while the patient is under anaesthesia. It is usually administered by a team of trained medical professionals who include a psychiatrist, an anaesthesiologist, and a nurse, and is only for people who are very depressed and may be suicidal. Usually, it is prescribed in circumstances where medications have not worked or for people who have experienced bad side effects from medications.

Treatments are usually given two to three times a week for three to six weeks, and approximately 80% of people with depression who receive ECT report an improvement in their mood and functionality.

Glenn was an inpatient at St John of God Hospital for over a month. He received three rounds of ECT each week with a general anaesthetic injection. After a month, he came home and continued treatment as an outpatient twice a week. He had 17 rounds of ECT, and after each treatment he would have a sore jaw and muscles from spasms that occurred during the treatment, but nothing worked. He was not improving at all, and in fact was getting worse. Yvette and Glenn didn't know what else to do.

One day Glenn's mother took him to his appointment instead of Yvette. The psychiatrist had booked Glenn in for more ECT treatment, and Yvette called him and asked why he was giving Glenn more ECT treatment when it hadn't worked. The psychiatrist was at a loss and said, "I don't know what else to do." This just didn't feel right at all, and later Yvette felt that she should have been stronger and said no. Glenn went on to have 12 more rounds of ECT, making it a total of 29, which was way too many. Whilst the number of sessions needed will vary, according to The Royal Australian and New Zealand College of Psychiatrists eight to 12 sessions are sufficient.

Glenn suffered serious side effects, one of which was that his memory deteriorated badly. One day he was working on his boat and looking for a metal tube. Yvette noticed he was looking through a toy box and said, "You're not going to find it there." An hour later she saw him looking through the kitchen drawers and said, "You're not going to find it there either." A little while later she found him out in the garden still looking for the little metal tube and repeated "You're not going to find it there either," and this became increasingly frequent. For years, because Glenn worked such long hours and never attended school events for the children, Yvette's friends would ask "Who is this imaginary husband of yours?" When he stopped working and was having his ECT treatment he began to come to school events, even though he couldn't remember them afterwards.

Glenn also received ketamine infusions. Ketamine is a psychedelic drug used for treatment-resistant depression - that is for severe depression that has not improved with other therapies. Ketamine has been shown to provide relief, particularly for people considering suicide, and it can be lifesaving, although it is usually a treatment of last resort due to a lack of long-term research into its benefits and side effects, which include dizziness, headaches, blurred vision, and nausea. Glenn would go into hospital for a 24-hour ketamine infusion and feel good. He would say "Oh my God, this is working," but it would last for about a week and then he would crash badly. This happened every month. He loved the highs but couldn't handle the lows. As with everything else Glenn had tried, ultimately ketamine didn't work either.

Ketamine use in Australia has increased recently. Between 2016-2019 its use went from 0.4% to 0.9% of the population, and during COVID-19 lockdowns, its use by people who regularly use drugs rose by 21%. There is a big difference between legal ketamine used in medical settings and illegal recreational use to get high. Medical ketamine is highly regulated and of better quality, and illegal ketamine carries significantly more risks because you don't know what you're taking. The most famous case of death relating to ketamine use was that of Friends star Matthew Perry. He was given ketamine as the key treatment for depression and anxiety in a clinic and became addicted. His needs were then met by unscrupulous doctors and a network of street dealers. The day he died he had had three injections of ketamine, and in the three days before he died, his assistant had injected him with it six times each day. My point is that ketamine is a strong drug which clearly creates a wonderful high for many people, but sadly for us the positive effects were not sustainable and did not reduce Glenn's depression, which got worse, and its impact on Yvette and the children became too much for them to bear.

Eventually Yvette and Glenn separated in 2011. It was simply too hard for Yvette to endure the struggles of the relationship and his increasingly depressed moods any longer. She loved Glenn dearly but could not go on living with it all. Although I really liked Glenn - everyone did - I agreed it was best for Yvette. I could see that this unhealthy pattern was making her unhappy, and she had become snappy, frustrated, and was no longer the kind, compassionate, empathetic, and caring person she had always been. She needed to get her life back together again.

I was amazed and so happy for her as I watched my sister transform her life following the separation. Gradually over the years, Yvette had put on weight. She was not fit or healthy. She had taken care of everyone else but neglected to take care of herself. When Glenn and Yvette split up, this changed. She decided to change her health radically and went to personal training sessions with a wonderful PT called Connie. She loved feeling fit and strong and became addicted. The more she trained, the better she felt and the more she wanted that feeling to continue. She had never been into sport or done anything so physical in her life. I remember her asking me one day "Why didn't you tell me how amazing it is when you get an endorphin rush?" I had felt this level of euphoria many times, but for Yvette it was a totally new and wonderful sensation. As she became fitter, she changed her eating habits and began choosing healthier options. The weight started to fall off her, and she lost 30kgs in 12 months. She looked great and her vitality and energy came back. She became Connie's pin-up girl, and when Connie couldn't run one of her PT sessions, she occasionally asked Yvette to step in. Yvette loved that so much that she decided to become a personal trainer herself and completed her certificates 3 and 4 in fitness. For a while she worked for Connie, getting up around 5am to hold classes. This was unheard of for Yvette who had always been a night owl, and I never thought I would see her get up so early. She set up a home gym arrangement and started running her own PT sessions with her own clients from home. It was wonderful to see her happy again and leading a much more fulfilling life.

Yvette and Glenn remained close friends despite their separation, which was quite emotional and very sad, but reasonably amicable. Yvette still loved Glenn even though she had come to terms with the fact that she couldn't live with him. Somehow Glenn seemed to understand that Yvette needed to move on, and didn't hold her leaving him against her. They managed to agree on how to look after the children together - all three lived with Yvette, but stayed with Glenn on a semi-regular basis, usually one night a week and every second weekend, unless he was not well and could not look after them.

But Glenn continued to go downhill. He could only work sporadically on projects where if he didn't turn up, it didn't really matter. By this time, it seemed too late for his mental health to improve. He had tried so many treatments, from medications to ECT and counselling. It seemed that he had had a small window of opportunity when he left work the first time, but after he went back to work in the family business he never recovered.

In April 2017, Glenn decided to go off all medication and give up smoking. He wanted to get all the poisons out of his body. Ironically, he said he wanted to do it to be more awake for his children, but this was the beginning of the end because he went to a whole new level of low, and became psychotic, which he hadn't been in the past. One night he stayed at his sister Cherryn's place, but he couldn't sleep. Cherryn tried to help him, but he thought that if he went to sleep, he would never wake up.

In June 2017, Glenn ended up in the psychiatric ward in Dandenong Hospital. Their 16-year-old daughter Jess was about to go to India for 24 days with World Challenge through her school, and Yvette wanted to take Jess to see Glenn before she left, but he said "No, I don't want her to see me like this." Yvette said, "Jess needs to see you before she goes to have peace of mind," and he replied "No, I don't want her to see me all battered and bruised." "What do you mean?" Yvette asked. He said, "Maybe you should talk to Cherryn." Yvette called Cherryn, who told her the day before he had tried to hang himself. He was taken to hospital because he was suicidal, and they had left him alone in a small cubicle in the emergency ward with access to tubes and cords. He was hanging when the curtain rail broke and he fell and hit his face, which was all bruised and swollen.

He went into hospital on the Monday, and Yvette found out about his attempted suicide on Tuesday. She had arranged for Glenn to pick Jess up from school on the Monday, but he called Yvette and said, "I'm sorry I can't pick Jess up because I'm in hospital." Yvette picked Jess up, who asked "Where is Dad? Why didn't he pick me up?" Yvette told her he was in hospital, and Jess asked, "Is he suicidal?" Yvette said she didn't know, and that that Glenn had been drugged, and then tripped and fallen over.

Jess sensibly knew it was a possibility. Yvette was honest in her response, although when she did later find out he had attempted to take his life, she didn't want to tell Jess the truth because she didn't want it to ruin her trip. She knew Jess would think about it a lot while she was away on the trip of a lifetime.

In early July, Glenn was discharged from hospital after only eight days. Initially he stayed with Cherryn, but he did not get better, and a couple of weeks later he was readmitted. By this time Jess had returned from India, and Yvette rang the doctors and asked if she could take him out for a few hours so that the kids didn't have to see him in the psychiatric ward - not a very nice place for children to see their father. They went to the Pancake Parlour, and he asked to speak to them privately, although he was not making much sense. After taking him back to hospital, Tim, who was 18, said to Yvette "I looked down at Dad's shoes, and instead of laces he had tape wrapped around them. I was going to ask why, and then it dawned on me." He had realised that when someone attempts to take their own life the hospitals don't allow them to wear shoelaces in case they use them to hang themselves.

Glenn returned home and had regular visits from the Peninsula Health Intensive Treatment Team, the team that helps look after mentally unwell patients once they have been discharged. So, he had support at home, although it wasn't enough.

On 9 August, Yvette and the children picked Glenn up and they went out for dinner at Dumplings Delish, a simple Asian restaurant. By then he was very unwell, and on 14 August Yvette called to check on him. Glenn was extremely low, and they spent an hour on the phone. Yvette was not able to continue working, so she cancelled the six clients scheduled for that afternoon and took him to see his psychiatrist. They sat in the car and chatted for half an hour because they were early. Glenn said that he was suicidal, and they went in for the appointment together. All options were discussed. Since ECT and ketamine were not working, and they agreed on a treatment called TMS (transcranial magnetic stimulation), which uses magnetic fields generated from an electrical coil placed over the scalp to activate specific areas of the brain. Over repeated sessions, the changes in brain activity are thought to correct abnormal brain functioning associated with depression.

Glenn was booked into a private psychiatric hospital ten days later to begin this new treatment, but in the car before his appointment he said "Please don't tell him I'm suicidal. I hate it in hospital, and he would put me back in there." Yvette decided to go against Glenn's wishes and explained that he was suicidal and asked the psychiatrist to prescribe something immediately, but he said "We need to wait until the TMS treatment" and decided not to give Glenn anything else until then. As they were driving home, Yvette suggested "Let's pick Jess up from hospital where she's doing work experience." They picked her up and did a few things together. They then dropped Glenn home and made sure he had everything he needed. It was the last time Yvette and Jess saw him alive.

Yvette called Jenny later that night and explained everything. She asked, "Did I do the right thing, or should I have made them put him in hospital to keep him safe even though I knew he hated it in there so much?" Jenny replied, "You did the right thing – he hated it in hospital, and he wouldn't have got better there."

One week later, on 21 August 2017, Jenny called Yvette, who didn't answer the phone because she was terrified of what she might hear, and she had 11-year-old Georgia and two of Georgia's friends in the car. Yvette dropped them at netball training, and then went straight home and into her bedroom so that Jess couldn't hear her, and rang Jenny who said, "He's done it, Yvette." Yvette stamped her foot several times saying "No, no, no!" and went into shock. She realised she had a personal training client coming in ten minutes, and tried to call her, but the client didn't answer so she had to text her to cancel their session, but her hands were shaking so much that she couldn't text properly.

Yvette went down the hallway to tell Jess but hadn't realised that Tim had come home while she was on the phone. He came up the hallway with a pile of dirty dishes in his hands, and she said, "Put the dishes down." He saw the look on her face and asked "What's wrong, Mum? You're scaring me," and she had to give him the devastating news that his dad had taken his life. How does a mother tell her children something like this that will change their lives forever? When she told him, he was totally shocked and gutted. They were hugging and crying. Then Yvette looked up and saw Jess standing there. She asked, "Is it Dad?" And Yvette replied "Yes." Jess had seen it coming. She came over in tears and joined in the family hug. Georgia was at netball training, and due to be dropped home in under an hour. Yvette called Mum, who came straight over. She called me too but asked that I come over the next day. Georgia got home, and Yvette asked her to sit down. She said, "Your Dad has taken his own life." Georgia didn't quite understand, and she said "Huh?" So, Yvette had to say it bluntly: "Your dad has killed himself."

Over the next few days, Jess wanted to know how he had killed himself. Yvette said "Darling, you don't want to know. It was horrendous." Jess said, "All the possibilities going through my head are going to be worse than knowing the truth," so Yvette reluctantly told Jess and the other kids the tragic circumstances, which I will not repeat here.

The impact on Yvette's family

The impact of Glenn's tragic life and his suicide on his family has been immense. It is six years since he died. At the time of his death, Georgia was 11, Jess 16, and Tim 18 years old. The daily harrowing toll has naturally faded somewhat with the passage of time, but it is like an emotional roller coaster. Although gradually the memories become a little less extreme, they never leave you after a trauma of that magnitude. Yvette has suffered from extreme sadness and guilt. The sadness is normal and totally understandable. She has been sad for many reasons. She is sad for Glenn's terrible pain over his last five to ten years, sad for her children and the effect it has had on them, sad for the tragic way he ended his life, sad to just recall all the terrible episodes Glenn had, and sad that his life and their life together didn't turn out better. This is a normal part of grieving, and it is healthy and helpful to go through this grieving process. Sometimes we just need to sit with the sadness and the discomfort it causes and allow ourselves to feel these emotions as we mourn. To feel positive emotions like joy, we also need to be able to feel sorrow.

Notwithstanding this, I have often thought of Yvette's guilt, and I can't think of any positive outcome from this emotion. Guilt is the belief that you did a bad thing, and Yvette's guilt has been largely caused by her belief that she should not have left Glenn. In other words, she did a bad thing. She still loved him but couldn't cope with living with him anymore. I believe it was the right thing for her to do, but it doesn't matter what I believe. It only matters what Yvette believes. She blames herself for his death, although intellectually she understands it was not her fault.

She still has some nagging doubts: "If I hadn't left him, would he be alive today?" "Should I have stayed with him?" "Could I have done more for him?" "Should I have done more for him?"

I have watched Yvette beat herself ever since Glenn died. She has cried for days, weeks, months, and years, but I wonder what else she feels. Does she also feel regret, which is all about having unmet expectations, and feeling that she in some way she caused the loss of a human life? I certainly believe that Yvette takes too much personal responsibility for many things that are not her fault. She felt responsible for many of Glenn's complex issues, and probably extremely frustrated too because she was not able to fix them. She no doubt felt a level of helplessness and despair about the entire situation, and of course the inconsolable grief due to his loss. Over time she has adapted to the grief, but it will never go away.

As a psychologist with a cognitive behavioural background, I believe the aim in this situation should be to learn which emotions are normal and healthy, and which are unhelpful, and over time seek to reduce the unhelpful emotions and develop the more helpful and positive ones. A key starting point would be to learn to become an "emotion scientist". This requires you to be sensitive to your emotions, and to begin by labelling them accurately. Typically, we only use a few words to describe how we feel (e.g. I feel good or bad). In the previous paragraphs I used a range of words including sadness, grief, guilt, regret, frustration, despair, and helplessness. Once we learn to label how we feel accurately, we can seek to understand what causes us to feel this way. While situations such as the death of a loved one can trigger certain feelings, it is our thoughts that ultimately cause us to feel emotions. As an emotion scientist, we need to learn about how our thoughts are contributing to or directly causing us to feel a certain emotion such as guilt. Once we begin to understand the patterns of thoughts that cause our emotions, we can either seek to let go of those thoughts or change them. Emotions such as sadness and grief from a tragic loss are normal and unavoidable. In fact, if you didn't feel this way based on my story, that would be unusual and probably a sign that something was not quite right in you. Being able to feel sadness means that you are emotionally moved by an event, and if you can't feel sadness, you may also not be able to feel joy. Whereas feeling guilty is an emotion directly caused by the thoughts Yvette has about the circumstances surrounding Glenn's death. Guilt is not a useful emotion and will not help Yvette or the people around her in any way. The challenge for Yvette - and the others - is how to change. Unfortunately, there is no magic wand, and it takes time and deliberate practice, just like learning a physical skill. This is a mental skill. One of my favourite people in the world is the Dalai Lama. He has been practising this since he was chosen at the age of four, and it takes a lifetime of practice. Specifically, you need to note your emotions, labelling them accurately, understanding the thoughts that lead to them, and finding ways to either let them go or change them. Over time you can change your thinking and teach yourself to have more helpful and constructive thoughts, which ultimately lead you to feeling more consistently better. Hopefully, my sister can learn to do this and let go of some of the unhelpful negative emotions that she is still holding on to. I love her dearly, and I would like her to have more genuine happiness and fewer negative emotions.

I have also been shaken to observe how this has affected Yvette's children. Clearly the loss of their father by suicide was a tragic event. In 1969, Swiss psychologist Elizabeth Kubler-Ross classified different emotions and thoughts people typically go through after losing someone they love. These are known as the five stages of grief. Since then, two additional stages have been added and so there are now seven stages of grief. These stages are not always perfect, and the process of grief is non-linear and much messier than a simple seven-stage model, but regardless of the order of your emotional experience, the key point is that grieving for the loss of a loved one is normal and healthy. It is necessary to allow yourself to grieve, heal, and work your way through your emotional journey rather than trying to avoid your grief. While people may experience them in a different order, the usual emotions following grief are:

> Shock and disbelief, denial, guilt, anger and bargaining, depression, loneliness and reflection, reconstruction (or working through) and acceptance.

We all felt a strong sense of shock and disbelief when we found out about Glenn's suicide. Initially it was impossible to even comprehend what had happened. I know Yvette felt guilt for a long time. It is normal to wonder what you could have done to prevent the loss (e.g. "I should have done more"). At some point anger and bargaining would have surfaced as the predominant emotion. This usually happens after the funeral, when you try to move on and get on with your life, and you might start angry with the doctors. For example, why did the psychiatrist give Glenn 29 rounds of ECT? Anger may be directed at Glenn being selfish to take his own life, but this maladaptive feeling can lead to prolonging the stage of guilt. Deep sadness and depression usually follow the sense of anger. You regularly feel lonely and isolated. Mental health advisors usually suggest this is the time to seek professional help through a grief counsellor. I know that Yvette, Tim, Jess, and Georgia have all done this at various times with different levels of success. The final stage of grief is acceptance. If you can work through the painful emotions I've described, you can usually get to a point of accepting your loved one is gone and that you need to get on with your life. You may even smile when you think of your loved one rather than cry.

The rate of suicide for people with mood disorders such as depression and bipolar disorder is estimated to be 25 times higher than in the general population. A staggering 65,000 Australians attempt suicide, and over 3,000 – more than eight a day - of them succeed each year. This is double the road toll, and yet it is not something we talk about.

The 2020-22 National Study of Mental Health and Wellbeing showed that one in six Australians aged 16-85 had seriously thought about taking their own life; over 7% had made a suicide plan, 5% had attempted suicide, and 36% of Australians were close to someone who took or attempted to take their life. For me, this last point is terribly important because it says that one in three of us knows someone who has tried, successfully or not, to take their own lives. Once again, this is rarely discussed. It's like it is a taboo subject. We need to talk about these shocking statistics more openly to reduce the stigma and to help our loved ones to work through their pain and suffering. Often people considering suicide are dealing with a combination of mental ill-health and difficult watersheds. Researchers believe that some people who end their lives do not actually want to die, but feel they have no other option to relieve their pain. Some may feel hopeless and that things will not get any better. I certainly believe that is how Glenn felt, and that he wanted to be released from his distress.

People who take their own lives sometimes show warning signs beforehand as Glenn did. His symptoms escalated, he expressed hopelessness, his bizarre behaviours increased, and he withdrew from friends and family. Some people begin to put their affairs in order, which Glenn also did, and others either write, speak, or joke about suicide.

If you think someone is at risk, it is important to talk with them supportively, giving them an opportunity to discuss their distress, and to encourage them to get professional help. Yvette and Glenn did all these things, but none were effective in the end. Glenn's pain was clearly too great, and he felt that he had no other plausible option. Rest in peace, Glenn.

The last few years with Q

—

As Q aged, he gradually spent less time in P Block. This doesn't mean he got better but was due to several factors: he became more aware of when he was becoming unwell and to understand this aspect of himself, and so as a result he would sometimes voluntarily admit himself to Monash Psychiatric Ward. This meant he was in better shape than perhaps he had been when he was admitted as an involuntary patient, so he didn't stay in hospital as long. He also had better support living in the community. NDIS was very good for Q.

Notwithstanding this, Q's delusions and paranoia never left him. He still wanted to go back to Israel. In his mind, the trip had been a success and gone smoothly, and even though he acknowledged that I had gone to Bangkok to save him, he was convinced that the next trip would be an even greater success. However, we had learnt from that experience. We had taken his passport away again and called the Australian Passport Offices as further insurance and told them never to grant him another passport, and we asked them to put a note in their filing system so that this was recorded somewhere officially. We made sure we had control of his money and that he couldn't get access to enough to pay for another ticket. None of this alleviated his obsession with Israel and more broadly with religion. At times he thought he was Jesus. Q would attend family functions dressed all in white: he had white tennis shoes, white pants and a white shirt. He looked like he was ready for a game of cricket, and yet he dressed like this because he thought this made him pure and free from guilt or sin.

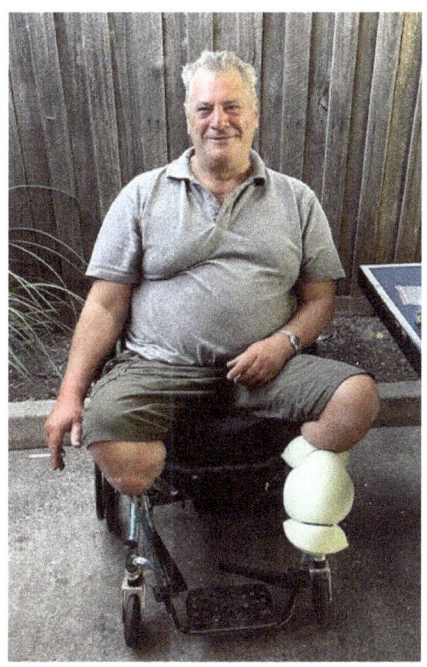

Q – with cigarette in hand in his standard position just outside his front door in an open undercover area

Q continued to have dark thoughts about his neighbours killing people, and became less physically active, often spending entire days sitting in his wheelchair in his front courtyard smoking endless cigarettes and doing his "work". Usually, he didn't like us asking him about his "very important work", but when we did manage to discuss it he would say "I am helping my people." He would concentrate, and he could talk with them telepathically and send them messages of support. I'm not quite sure if he was able to stop their pain and suffering or just sent messages of love to them. Perhaps this work gave him some sense of satisfaction because it gave him meaning and purpose. I'm not sure but I hope so.

I enjoyed painting with Q. We spent about three hours together once every month or two. I would arrive at his unit in Clayton, and Q would not have anything ready, although he would be mentally prepared. There was a table tennis table that he used to sit at most days under cover in his little courtyard, regardless of the weather or the time of year - even on the coldest days in the middle of winter. When I arrived, I would begin to get the equipment out: the paints, paint brushes, water, and he had large pads of thick paper that we used. I need to make it clear that my artistic skills are very limited, and Qs were worse than mine. However, it didn't matter at all. Q thought that I was incredibly talented and that I had a gift. I didn't have the heart to tell him otherwise. He usually had a theme in mind for our paintings. Some of them were quite normal, and others were weird and unusual. For example, once we had to paint a picture with different tennis-related objects, whereas on another occasion we had to paint objects that depicted Q's "big nose", which he felt he had. I arrived one day, and he had a very clear view of what we would paint: an image of the four elements – fire, air, earth, and water. Sometimes we would paint separate pictures, and other times we would create one together, sharing the painting. Qs were a little more abstract than mine. Of course, this was not about the painting at all. It was about two brothers spending quality time together, interacting and enjoying themselves. For Q, it was a brief period of respite from whatever else was going on in his mind.

Whilst we had been focusing on Q's mental health for years, we were aware that his physical health was declining. He used to smoke about 60 cigarettes per day. He would smoke quickly too, breathing the smoke in rapidly, blowing it out swiftly, and taking another drag. He certainly didn't give the impression he enjoyed the cigarette. It was a terrible habit that we knew one day would cause him dreadful pain and problems, and he knew that his smoking was probably killing him, but he also seemed to understand that he was powerless to stop himself. He tried giving up on several occasions but failed. He would last for a few days or a week or slightly more, but he always started again. Sometimes he tried to cut down and smoke less. This worked for a little while, and there were times where he managed to only smoke about 25 cigarettes per day. Unfortunately, it wouldn't last, and he would creep up again to his usual 60. He tried hypnotherapy once, but it didn't seem to work for him. Mum went on talking about it, even though it hadn't worked. He tried nicotine patches too, but nothing seemed to help. He had developed many bad habits and was not strong-minded enough to change.

When Q was young, he was extremely fit and healthy and took a great deal of exercise. However, in his later years he hardly moved. Occasionally Yvette and I would encourage him to go for a wheel around the block, and this sometimes worked. Or we would go together, but usually he didn't feel like it. When Yvette was a personal trainer, she brought over boxing gloves and some other gym equipment and he liked that, but it never became a habit.

Q – one of our best photos of him all dressed up at a wedding

Q's eating habits were atrocious too, and he would not accept any feedback or advice. He loved cheese, pasta, and potatoes, and would eat a lot of pasta or potatoes with a huge quantity of melted cheese on top. Most of the time Q was a vegetarian, unless he changed his mind which happened from time to time. This was mostly good for him, but he didn't get enough protein. Perhaps the worst thing was how fast he ate. Q would demolish his food like an animal, gulping mouthfuls and swallowing his food without chewing it more than about three or four times. It was hard to watch, and if I ate like that, I would be sick.

So, it was not surprising when he began to have serious health problems. In October 2021, Q called Yvette saying, "I'm in agony." He had complained about stomach pains many times, but it was hard to tell how real they were. Yvette spent several hours in the emergency ward of Monash Hospital with him, and told the doctors "He has schizophrenia, and I'm not sure if this pain is real or in his mind." For some reason they did not do any blood tests. They examined his stomach, but the additional pressure was not painful. He was given morphine, which he loved. It gave him a wonderful high and relieved the pain. Shortly after this they sent him home with no diagnosis or treatment beyond the morphine.

Q's GP was a nice man, which is why he went on seeing him, but as we got more involved, we realised he was not very competent and had been prescribing pain medication for many years without seeking the cause of the problem. He gave Q a form for a blood test on one occasion, but Q never had the test, and the GP kept giving him medication without delving any deeper. Had they done more thorough testing and diagnosis, they would have found out that he had hyponatraemia, an illness where the level of sodium in the blood is too low, so the body holds too much water. When the water levels rise, the cells swell up causing nausea, vomiting, headaches, confusion, fatigue, restlessness, muscle weakness, and stomach pains. Q also had something called polydipsia, so that he was very thirsty however much he drank. He was drinking 10-12 litres of fluid a day, and consuming a variety of drinks including diet coke, water, cordials, coffee, and iced tea. His hands were puffy and swollen, but we thought that was because he was overweight. When he smoked, he often dropped his cigarette, and I supposed he was either losing his co-ordination or distracted and simply let go of his cigarette, but now I think it was because of his hyponatraemia and swollen fingers.

Q was beginning to have trouble breathing, leading to many hospitalisations for physical health issues. On 18 January 2022, he had a cardiac arrest. Clare had been with him from 9am to midday at his unit in Clayton, and he had complained again about stomach pain. When she left, she called Yvette to talk about his medications, but when Yvette tried to ring him, and he didn't answer all afternoon she began to worry. Yvette rang me and Mum, but he did not answer our calls either, so Yvette got in her car and drove the 20 minutes to his home, where her fears turned to reality when she found him in a catatonic state. He could not move normally, but he was breathing although not well. He did not respond to Yvette and had lost control of his bladder so his clothes, his wheelchair, the floor, and his bed were all very wet. Yvette was unsure whether his catatonic state was psychological or physical. Frequently the inability to move normally is associated with schizophrenia and/or other mental illnesses, but there may also be lack of speech and other unusual behaviours. She rang the Crisis Assessment and Treatment Team (CATT), a group of mental health professionals who include psychiatric nurses, social workers, psychiatrists, and psychologists, and whose main role is to provide immediate help during a mental health crisis. We had got to know the CATT team reasonably well over the years and Yvette assumed that they would be helpful, but on this occasion, they were not as due to his combined mental and physical health issues they felt Q was not in their domain. Yvette immediately rang an ambulance, which arrived within ten minutes.

When she rang me, I realised this was a major emergency and drove straight to Q's place and got there shortly after the ambulance.

There were two female and a male paramedic, all very understanding, who dealt with the situation with a professional calm that was a credit to them, and disarming for us. I could see Q sitting in his wheelchair, eyes open and yet still unresponsive. The paramedics were trying to get him into the ambulance. They had pushed him in his wheelchair to the ambulance trolley, however because he was not able to help and was extremely heavy, they were not able to get him onto the trolley. They took a board out and put it between his wheelchair and the trolley, but for this to work they needed Q to help. He simply could not move himself along the board and onto the trolley though, and the paramedics had run out of ideas and were talking about calling in a second ambulance. At that stage I was very fit and strong, and suggested that I carry him with Yvette helping. They were not keen, but I was getting desperate, and Q needed to get to hospital quickly, so without waiting for their approval and with Yvette's help I lifted Q up and onto the trolley, making sure to keep my back straight so I didn't injure myself. It worked, and I went to the hospital in the ambulance while Yvette stayed and cleaned up a bit before joining me there.

By the time Yvette arrived, I was sitting outside the emergency department. Due to COVID restrictions, we could not both be with him as initially they only allowed one person at a time to be with a patient. Yvette went in and spoke to the triage nurse, who realised this was a possible life and death situation and said we could come in together. However, we were not taken to see Q, but into a small room nearby. We were wondering what was going on and feared that this was the end. I thought it might be a room where they take you to deliver bad news, but then a nurse and a doctor came in and told us that Q was still unresponsive. His heart had stopped beating and he had had a cardiac arrest, so they had given him cardiopulmonary resuscitation (CPR), and he was now on life support. Effectively, he was being kept alive by a machine that was helping him breathe. I remember Yvette and I sitting next to each other in this small room with two bright red couches. We were listening intently to every word the doctor and nurse were saying, holding hands and trembling slightly. We both knew this was a big moment in our lives and for Q. The doctor and nurse were kind, solicitous, and sympathetic as they sat opposite us. Leaning forward gently, the doctor asked us the toughest question of our lives "If Q has another cardiac arrest and his heart stops, do you want us to resuscitate him again?" By this time Yvette and I were both in tears. It had all happened so fast, and we had never discussed this with Mum or Q. The doctor and nurse left us to talk about it, and we discussed the pros and cons of keeping him alive. Q had very little quality of life. He was existing, but there was no joy. He had told us many times that he didn't want to live, so we thought it wasn't fair to keep him alive even though we would be devasted. We didn't have time to consult Mum, but we knew she could not make the decision. It would be too difficult for a mother to decide what to do with her son. The doctor and nurse returned a few minutes later, and I said, "If his heart stops again, we will not resuscitate him." They nodded their understanding, and agreed it was the right decision given all the circumstances. They were supportive and could see our anguish.

Q was moved to the Intensive Care Unit (ICU) still on life support and stayed there for a week. A ventilator attached to a tube that was inserted down into his airway via his throat forced air into his lungs. He gradually improved, and after about a week he was moved into another ward. Then about a week later he was discharged and went home. We were happy that Q had recovered, but realised that he could no longer look after himself, and decided he needed to move into a supported residential service (SRS) accommodation and looked at several on the internet and then made appointments to visit the ones that seemed the most suitable. We took Q to a few, and together we selected the place that we all thought would be best. Q was quite reluctant to leave his home for an SRS arrangement. He loved his independence at home, but he also had enough self-awareness to realise he needed help daily, and we could not provide this level of care. His needs were much more constant than they had been, and we had been told by the doctors that he had Chronic Obstructive Pulmonary Disease (COPD), which is a lung disease that causes restrictive airflow. He might have another cardiac arrest and needed close monitoring to ensure he would not be alone.

We eventually agreed on his moving to a place called Hampton House, which was exactly what Q needed. The staff were friendly, kind, and considerate, and they genuinely cared about all the patients. He was served three meals per day and enjoyed the food. It was great that he didn't have to cook for himself anymore. It was all quite basic, but ideal for Q's needs, and only five minutes from my home so I was able to visit him regularly, which he liked. Sometimes I would take him out for a few hours or bring him home for a while.

One of our favourite things was to buy fish and chips and drive down to Green Point, near Brighton Beach. We would sit in my car with the windows open, looking out over Port Phillip Bay and all the way to the city. The view was always calming, and we would eat our fish and chips and reminisce about the "good old days". Q loved it and so did I, but when I took him back to Hampton House, I would feel sad, despite the lovely time we had spent together, because of his significant deterioration, and to see the state of the other patients living there. Most of them had severe intellectual and/or physical disabilities, and many had lived there for years. I remember walking into Hampton House for the first time. It was shortly after 5pm, and the patients were all in the dining room having dinner. They offered Q some dinner too and he said yes. As he sat down to eat, Yvette and I sat down too and talked to some of the patients. The ones who were well enough to engage in conversation were delightful. There were two women in their early fifties who clearly had an intellectual disability but were keen to chat with us. They invited us to sit down at their table, and after we told them we were thinking about Hampton House for our brother, they began telling us all about their experience. They loved it. They told us about themselves, and how friendly the staff were. This was like a little interview for us, hearing directly from the patients that they were satisfied with the place. Their existence wasn't fantastic, nonetheless it was safe and sociable. That was what Q needed. He occasionally went home to his unit in Clayton, which we had kept just in case things didn't work out at Hampton House, but he ended up living at Hampton House on and off for about eight months.

Following Q's near-death experience, we had several uncomfortable yet necessary discussions with him about whether he wanted to live. We spoke about his quality of life, and then the circumstances in which he would not want to live. We decided to organise an advance care plan for Q. An advance care plan is the process of discussing and choosing future health care and medical treatment options, where people make decisions about their medical treatment including future consent, refusal or withdrawal of treatment. In August 2022, after Q's second cardiac arrest and only a few weeks before he passed away, Yvette and I arranged a meeting with a lovely lady called Sharon from Alfred Health to draft an advanced care plan for Q. Sharon was caring and sympathetic in her approach, and she helped to make the conversation much less awkward than it might have been. It was a meeting over Zoom. Q and Yvette came to my home, and we sat at the kitchen table with Q in the middle and Yvette and I on either side of him. Whilst Yvette and I helped where necessary, Sharon directed all her questions to Q. We had already had several conversations with Q to explain what the meeting was all about and to help him think about his wishes in advance. Sharon asked Q about his personal values, goals, and preferences for treatment and care, and at one point, the conversation took a funny turn. Sharon asked Q what gave him pleasure. He responded in a way that I wasn't expecting, saying that he "enjoyed sex and smoking." We knew that he enjoyed smoking, but I was not prepared for him to say sex was one of his top two pleasures. Although he didn't have a girlfriend and had never had one, we knew that he had visited sex workers from time to time. We did not judge him on this, because we all wanted him to have some happiness and pleasure in his short life. Sharon didn't seem to be surprised by this comment as she simply restated what he had said and probed a little bit to fully understand his wishes. She then said she would draft an advance care plan and send it to us to review and sign. The key decision in this document was that if Q had another cardiac arrest, he did not want to be resuscitated, but for this document to be legally binding, Q needed to sign it.

In June 2022, five months after his first episode and a month after our meeting with Sharon, Q had another cardiac arrest. I was in Bali on holiday with my family. Given his hyponatraemia and polydipsia, we had tried to work with the staff at Hampton House to limit his drinking. Along with his COPD, the 10-12 litres of fluid per day he drank were reducing the sodium levels in his blood, which led to him retaining too much water, resulting in the swelling of his cells, and ultimately contributing to his stomach pains. By this stage, we had changed Q's GP and arranged for a blood test to check his sodium levels. When the doctor saw the results of his blood test, he called Sari at Hampton House and said, "Take him to hospital immediately." Sari called a taxi, and Q went to Sandringham Hospital with a staff member, where he was instantly admitted to the emergency ward. By now he had become catatonic again and was awake yet non-responsive. The staff didn't realise this was not normal for Q, and a nurse gave him a sandwich. Q ate it too fast. He took huge mouthfuls and scoffed it down as usual without chewing properly, then choked, and he had another cardiopulmonary arrest. The doctors and nurses ran into his hospital room and performed CPR to resuscitate him again. They were not aware of his hyponatremia and hospital admissions five months earlier, because it was a different hospital. Nor did they know about his advance care plan, because it had not been signed and given to all local hospitals.

This all happened so fast that neither Mum nor Yvette was at the hospital, and when Yvette called, she was given different explanations as to what was going on. She was told that Q had gone into cardiac distress, that they had performed CPR and intubated him (put him on life support), and that they were in the process of transferring him to the Alfred Hospital because they didn't have an ICU. When Yvette arrived at the hospital, she saw Q hooked up to all sorts of tubes and machines to keep him alive, and a team of about eight hospital staff all performing various tasks. He was about to be transferred by ambulance to the Alfred Hospital, and Yvette hugged and kissed him, crying as she said goodbye, not knowing if she would see him alive again. Yvette and Mum went to see him in the ICU at the Alfred Hospital the next day and talked to the doctors about our previous decision not to resuscitate him.

In Victoria you can make a Do-Not-Resuscitate (DNR) order, which essentially instructs health care providers not to do CPR if a patient stops breathing or if their heart stops beating. Due to our decision during his cardiac arrest in January not to resuscitate him if he stopped breathing again, and after talking to the doctors about his extremely low quality of life and his desire not to continue living, we had activated the DNR order, but at Monash Hospital. Whilst Sandringham and the Alfred Hospital are connected, they are not able to see the Monash Hospital records, and the doctors at the Alfred, did not know about the DNR order. When Yvette explained, the doctors didn't seem to understand as Q was only 53 years old, and Yvette and Mum debated whether to call me. On the one hand, they didn't want to ruin my holiday in Bali, but on the other Yvette was struggling to decide what to do. Yvette wanted Mum's support, but Mum was too emotional to decide. She said, "As a mother I can't decide, but I would never hold it against you if you decided not to resuscitate him." This was simply too much for Yvette, but in the end, they didn't call me, and Q recovered.

Q's quality of life continued to go downhill, and he was admitted to hospital three times over the next three months. On one occasion he was struggling to breathe, so he was taken to Monash Hospital by ambulance. After a short stay in the emergency ward, he was transferred to a ward for people with dementia. It was a locked ward as patients would wander around, not knowing what they were doing or where they were going. Q hated being in hospital, and had developed several perverse, manipulative strategies for escaping. He asked a nurse if he could go downstairs to the cafeteria to buy a newspaper. Q never read the papers, but of course the nurse didn't know that, so she said yes. He pulled the drip out of his arm, got in his wheelchair, took the elevator down to the ground floor and proceeded to wheel himself home - about a kilometre. The nurses had no idea, but when Q got home, he telephoned Yvette and said, "Guess what, I outsmarted them, and I snuck out!" When Yvette called the hospital to tell them, the nurse said "No, he is in his room." But when they went to check, they realised the error they had made. Yvette was busy with another appointment, so her partner Damian drove over to pick Q up and took him to Hampton House to recover.

During another visit to hospital when he had chest x-rays because he was complaining of chest pain, they found several broken ribs and a broken sternum. The sternum is the long, flat bone in the centre of the chest which is connected to the ribs with cartilage. It forms the front of the rib cage, protecting the heart, lungs and other major blood vessels. Most sternal fractures are caused by direct trauma to the chest. When you have a fractured sternum, breathing becomes painful, and the pain normally gets worse when taking a deep breath, coughing or laughing. We realised that it must have been caused by the CPR treatment in June to resuscitate him. The pressure applied to the chest when giving CPR is enormous and had broken his sternum. It must have been agony, especially when he used his arms and upper body to get from his wheelchair onto the toilet, bed, car, or couch. He hardly complained though and was incredibly tough and resilient.

In between hospitalisations, Q went back to live at Hampton House. Clare continued to visit him twice a week and would either just spend time talking with him or take him out for a little while. He enjoyed that, and she continued to be supportive and caring. When she was there on 30 August 2022, she realised he was struggling to breathe again, and rang Yvette, who said to call an ambulance. It arrived within ten minutes, and Yvette phoned and told me he was on his way to Monash Hospital. Yvette's daughter Georgia had an important appointment, but Damian was able to jump in and help again, as he had repeatedly done, and took her. I was working but cancelled my meetings. It was early afternoon, and I raced to the hospital, wondering if this might be the end. I arrived to find Q in the emergency ward surrounded by about eight hospital staff, and being supported to breathe as he was not able to breathe by himself. I called Yvette and said, "Q is dying, please come quickly." She was already on her way. The doctors told us that the machines were keeping him alive, but only just. They also said this would keep happening and he would be back in a week or two if they saved him now. They knew of and accepted the advance care plan and the DNR order and stopped the treatment except for pain relief to make him as comfortable as possible. Yvette and I were in the room with him, holding his hand and crying as he passed away. I felt so many mixed emotions all at once. On the one hand I was grieving for him, but on the other I felt a sense of relief that his tortured life was finally over.

After sitting quietly with him for about 15 minutes, I decided that it was time we told Mum. I knew we should not tell her over the phone, so I left Yvette with Q and drove over to tell her in person. I called her from my mobile when I was about five minutes away, but I didn't tell her Q had passed away, just that I was coming to see her. I think she realised, but she only said "OK, I'll see you soon" quietly. When I arrived, I parked my car out the front like I always did and walked to the front door. I knocked, and Mum opened the door, looking at me with solemn eyes. I took her by the hand and led her to the couch in her living room a few metres away. Then I sat down with her and said gently "Q has passed away, Mum." She is a very stoic woman, my mother. We sat next to each other, holding hands and crying quietly together. There was no loud sobbing, just quiet, sad acknowledgement of this moment that we had known would come soon.

I drove Mum back the hospital to see Q. By the time we arrived, he had been moved to a small room so that we could be with him in our grief. Yvette, still deeply upset, was holding his hand, stroking his head, and occasionally kissing him on the forehead, struggling to let go. She wanted time to just be with him. Mum was totally different. She was so distressed that she couldn't stay in the room for more than ten minutes. It was too painful for her to see her son like this. It is unusual for a child to die before their parents, and whilst it was difficult for Yvette and me, it was terrible for Mum.

Then we called our children to tell them, and we all gathered at Mum's house that evening. We ordered pizzas and sat around comforting each other. My kids were wonderfully supportive. They all hugged me and gave me the love I needed to cope that night. It was important to have all our kids and immediate family together to help us grieve as one. We told stories about Q, and even managed several funny ones through our tears. It was cathartic.

Back to Craig and what's happening now

As I write this story about my family, I feel sad and somewhat nostalgic about the fact that Dad and Q have both died in the last two years, and Glenn six years ago. Glenn's death was tragic; Q's was exhausting, but ultimately a relief; Dad's was reasonably normal, and he had lived a good life. Now it is fascinating to reflect on the one person in this story who is still around – Craig. When I pause and consider his life, I am grateful for the recent positive changes. Craig is the happiest I have ever seen him at the ripe old age of 60. Since Dad passed away, Yvette and I, as executors of his will, have gradually been working through the complex distribution of his estate. Craig had been living in a house Dad owned in Langwarrin for the last 17 years. He loved the place, and he struggles with change, but we had to sell the house as part of Dad's estate administration, which meant that Craig had to move. This caused him a great deal of anxiety, but the good news is that the money Craig has received so far and will receive soon from the sale has been enough for him to buy a small unit and have enough money to lead a reasonably comfortable life from now on.

Craig initially wanted to buy a private unit nearby, but since he had never bought a house or anything anywhere near that price, he was not able to think it through clearly. His desires were all emotional and not logical or rational. Eventually we suggested he move into an over 55's community living arrangement, although he was not keen initially, thinking that it was for very old people and he was only just 60, and assuming it was like an old people's home. I sat down with him on several occasions, and patiently went through the pros and cons of a private unit compared to a community living arrangement, and Yvette and I slowly walked him through the financial scenarios for both. On paper, the community living situation looked better both financially and for his lifestyle, but he still wanted a private home because it felt better to him. I suggested we go and have a look at a few community living places, and said "We'll just look. You don't have to buy anything. Just look and see what you think, and then we'll talk about the options." I knew that he was likely to get emotionally attached to one of these places if it was any good. I had done my research and looked at all of them within a certain radius of where Craig wanted to live. I had found about eight places, made phone calls to each, and eventually whittled the list down to three good options. Yvette, Craig and I went to visit the first two and Craig fell in love with one. It was perfect for him.

So, late in 2023, we helped Craig move out of the house he had lived in for 17 years and into his new home. He loves it. In fact, this morning he sent me a random text message saying, "Thank you for all your help getting me this unit; I love it here." He has told me that about ten times in the last couple of weeks. It is so nice to see that he is happy, and we all made the right decision. There are many advantages to this arrangement. He has a unit that he owns, and he is very proud and pleased to finally own his own place. It has two bedrooms, so he has an additional room if he needs it. As part of the deal to buy the unit (technically it is a very long-term lease, but we don't need to go into those details), the owners totally gut and renovate it when the previous tenant leaves. Craig now has a recently redecorated unit that looks and feels new. The kitchen appliances are all new and he loves his kitchen. He has his own garage and a lovely little courtyard with a BBQ and table and chairs so he can sit outside. He has all he needs in terms of daily comforts and privacy. In addition to this, he has the support of a small community of about 100 people in a similar situation. Whilst there are some slightly older people in their seventies and even eighties, many are around his age. On Tuesday and Friday evenings they put on a pizza night or a fish and chips night. They all gather in the community centre, which is a handsome building only about 30 metres from Craig's unit. Craig likes his personal space and time alone, but he is also very sociable and loves the opportunity to build friendships and so this is the ideal situation for him. He can join in all the activities that they put on or spend time alone in his unit and has the best of both worlds. Yvette and I are also happy that his current and future safety and physical health needs are addressed. The community living place has a manager and a nurse on duty daily. If Craig falls or hurts himself, he can simply press a red button, someone will respond, and if necessary, an ambulance will be called. People are onsite who can immediately respond to his needs, which gives Yvette and me some peace of mind, knowing that as his physical health declines over the next decade, he will have the support he needs, rather than one of us having to drop everything and rush to his aid on a regular basis. He is not in that situation now but is likely to be at some point in the relatively near future.

With his new home secured and a girlfriend he cares about and who seems to care for him, Craig is the happiest I have ever seen him. He tells us regularly that he is extremely grateful for everything he has and for our support. No doubt he will have many more struggles and challenges, but for now he is content.

Housing, financial capacity and ageing

As I reflect on Craig's circumstances, planning for the later years of life, especially when you reach your sixties and beyond, is a complex endeavour that involves navigating both personal aspirations and systemic limitations. For those with sufficient financial capacity, this phase opens a variety of choices, ranging from comfortable retirement living options to investments in healthcare that ensure a quality life. However, even with financial readiness, the choices are not easy. Deciding where to live, how to maintain social connections, and managing health care requires thoughtful consideration and planning.

In Australia, one of the most pressing issues for the aging population is housing. The housing market does not cater to the needs of older adults, particularly those who are not homeowners and rely on renting. As property values continue to rise, affordable and appropriate rental options become scarce, which affects older renters disproportionately, and many find themselves in a precarious situation with limited options for more suitable housing.

From a societal perspective, the challenge of housing for the aging population is both systemic and urgent. It requires robust policy interventions that provide affordable housing solutions tailored to the needs of older adults. There's a clear need for a strategic approach that includes age-friendly housing policies, support for aging in place, and, perhaps most importantly, ensuring that the private rental market offers long-term security and affordability for older tenants.

On a more personal and human level, the uncertainties associated with aging evoke feelings from anxiety to resentment. Craig certainly experienced a heightened level of anxiety until we found a place that he loved. There is often a poignant sense of vulnerability as one faces increased dependence and the possibility of isolation. Compassion and understanding from the community and from policy makers play a vital role in easing these emotional burdens. Social supports and community services are crucial in ensuring that older adults feel valued and connected within their communities, and a compassionate approach involves acknowledging the diversity within the older population and recognising that everyone's needs and preferences vary significantly.

How has this shaped me personally and professionally?

Writing this book has been cathartic for me. In a slightly strange way, I have loved it. I have looked forward to sitting down and typing away. I think that is because it has forced me to pause and reflect on my life, and how it has been impacted by the stories I've told here. I certainly would not have become the person that I am today without these experiences. Over the years, when I have told some of these stories about Q, responses have frequently been "He is lucky to have a brother like you," and my immediate and honest response has been "I'm the lucky one; he is the one with the illness, and I am lucky to have been born and raised with the capacity to help him."

Every day for the last few years I have received a phone call from Craig. He usually calls me early, around 7am, because he knows I am an early riser, although not as early his usual 4:30 or 5am start to the day. He calls me on Facetime because he likes to see my face. It seems to help him read the social cues; he tells me. Sometimes I sleep in past 7am and his calls wake me up, so I recently asked him to text me first, and now I usually wake to a text asking, "Are you awake?" Craig will often call just to say hello, although usually he phones to tell me about a problem he has and ask for my advice or guidance. He jokingly says that I am his "psychologist on call". I usually answer his calls if I can, although sometimes there's a moment when I don't want to talk and have an urge not to respond, but then something pushes me to answer the phone. Perhaps I feel that it is an obligation, but I think it is more than that. We usually only chat for about five minutes. He is very respectful of my time and frequently says "I won't disturb you for too long, Hayden." He knows I lead a life that is fuller and busier than his, however I can see that he values our daily conversations.

Somehow, I believe that I am giving him five minutes of happiness. I am helping to provide a small window of joy for Craig, to calm down, to relax and solve his small but important daily challenges. In return, I am filled with compassion for him and his plight. The daily calls are a constant reminder of our very different lives, and they help me to realise my problems are minor in comparison to his. I usually have the skills and experience needed to deal with the challenges that life throws at me. Thinking about this reminds me of a great quote from Jim Rohn the American entrepreneur, author and motivational speaker: "*Don't wish for easier, wish you were better. Don't wish for less problems, wish for more skills. Don't wish for less challenge, wish for more wisdom.*"

I am grateful that I am reminded of this daily. Craig must work a lot harder to solve much simpler problems. Interestingly, his calls also make me feel loved, valued, respected, and appreciated - emotions that most of us want and need. In his later years, Craig has also become quite funny, or at least he laughs a lot, mostly at his own jokes, but his laughter is contagious. In this way, he inadvertently encourages me to be playful, silly, and happy.

Q used to call me every day too, until he passed away a little over 18 months ago. His calls were different. He didn't like to talk about himself too much. When I asked how he was, he would frequently respond with very short answers. I could usually tell if he was psychologically well or not by the silences on the other end. If Q was very unwell, we would have long periods of silence. This was a clear sign that his mind was elsewhere, and he was either hearing voices or a minor hallucination or delusion was going on in his brain. I would gently try to bring him back to the present reality, which sometimes worked. When he was better, he would ask how I was and have the capacity to listen and respond appropriately. Reflecting on these calls now makes me very sad, and I ask myself why I miss him so much. I used to call him and chat when I was driving somewhere. Now I often find myself driving along and thinking for a moment that I will call Q, until I realise, I can't talk to him again and feel a moment of grief. However, I think my sorrow is more than just missing my little brother; I believe it is regret for the life that he led and his struggles and his pain. It was mostly a life of suffering once he developed schizophrenia. Sure, there were some fun times, but not many.

Throughout Q's tragic life, I felt many different emotions, but mainly helplessness and hopelessness. I did my best to help him in small ways, but it never felt enough, which led to feelings of despair and discouragement at the unfairness of it all. But I would pull myself together and remind myself that life isn't fair. Life is about struggling and being OK with the struggle. After many of Q's episodes I felt numb, exhausted, and overwhelmed, so harrowed that I would turn to the problem-solving part of my brain during the event, whatever it was, to deal with the crazy situation that was unfolding. And then shortly after it was finished, I would fall in a heap, and cry, totally burned out. It was an emotional roller coaster. Yvette was usually with me, and we would hug each other and cry together.

Without these experiences, perhaps I would not have developed a such strong sense of care and compassion. Also, in a strange way I have felt that what I have gone through with my family has made me more resilient. I often see people struggle to cope with what I consider to be minor issues in comparison to my trials with Q and Craig, and I feel that I have perspective and appreciation of all the positive things in my life.

The last 37 years have given me greater perspective as far as my own problems are concerned and stop me from worrying too much. I repeatedly think of Maslow's Hierarchy of Needs model, which is usually represented as a pyramid, with the more basic needs at the bottom. Although the theory lacks conclusive supporting evidence, there is confirmation that the levels continuously overlap, and the lower stages do not have to be completely satisfied to move to a higher stage.

Maslow's Hierarchy of Needs Model

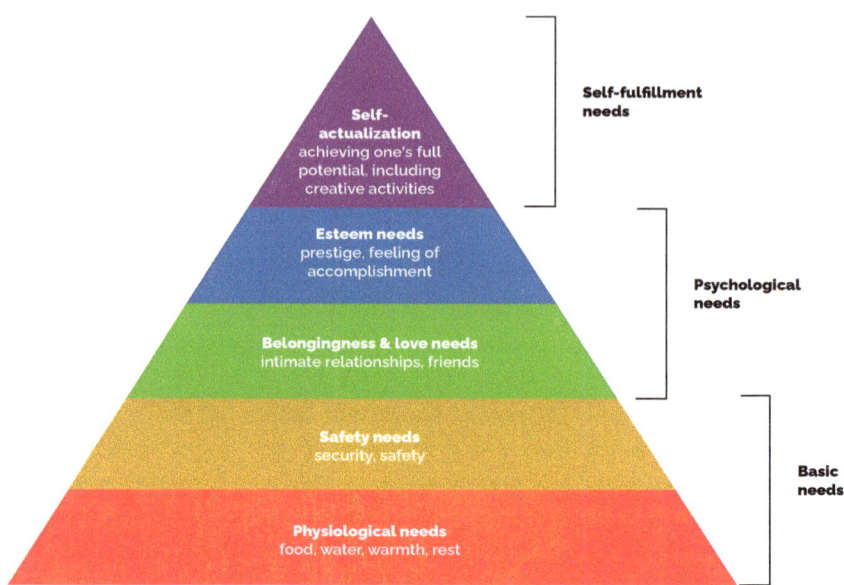

The theory concerns basic physiological needs such as food, water, and shelter. Q and Craig mostly had their physiological needs met, although frequently the quality of their food, clothes, and shelter was far below mine. The next level of need is for physical and psychological safety. The psychological safety needs usually relate to personal, emotional and financial security, and the goal of this need is stability and a state of homeostasis. Although Q and Craig were usually physically safe throughout their lives, they both lacked stability and security, particularly emotional security, so their daily struggles caused increased instability, and a great deal of emotional turmoil. Q's paranoia made him believe that he was in physical danger as were those around him, and his needs for psychological safety were certainly not met.

Love and social needs come next, and a sense of belonging. We all need to feel we belong to and are accepted within our social groups, but as Q got older, he gradually lost most of his friends. Some lovely people remained loyal and stayed with him throughout his life, but many fell away. Q always had more friends than Craig, who has had to learn to live with very few friends and often been alone and lonely. He has not known a sense of belonging, and his needs for love and social connection have seldom been met, which has contributed to his social anxiety and depression. Craig even turns up at family events in an anxious state and needs time to calm down and get comfortable in his new environment. I try to give him 10-15 minutes of time and space before speaking to him, because he has to adjust to a new situation, even if it is just family. This is particularly true at Christmas, when we are a large family, and this intimidates him.

Esteem is next in the hierarchy and involves respect from others and from oneself. This self-respect includes a need for strength, competence, independence, and mastery. Neither Q nor Craig had these qualities, which come from positive daily experiences where you gain a sense of your own competence.

The next levels of need are cognitive, such as creativity, foresight, and curiosity, aesthetic needs such as appreciation of beauty, and self-actualisation, the ability to realise your full potential.

The reason I habitually think of this model in relation to Q and Craig is that many people complain about things that are higher up the Hierarchy of Needs, and while those things may be real for them, they are perhaps not conscious of nor grateful for the fact that their basic needs for survival are being met. I am aware that I live in a beautiful home in a wealthy suburb in Australia. I have enough food, clothes, water, and sleep. I can buy myself a soy latte whenever I want. Although I don't always feel psychologically safe, I usually do. My health has usually been good, and my personal and financial security too. I am loved, and I have a strong sense of belonging with my friends and family. I have a job and a career that provide self-esteem and respect. I understand my own level of competence and mastery and am thankful for all of this. I have been aware of the disparity between me and my brothers for 40 years.

Beyond gratitude and resilience, my experiences have encouraged me to be more real and authentic. I am also comfortable being vulnerable and having the courage to take things on. I work in the corporate world where image is important, and where I see people who appear to be highly successful. I compare this environment to the world that my brothers inhabited for most of their lives, and the difference is vast, which brings me back down to earth. It grounds me and hopefully makes me a little bit humbler. It helps me to stay real and not to get above myself too often. It also allows me to be OK with discomfort. Many people want to push discomfort away, but I prefer to seek and take on challenges outside my comfort zone to grow and develop further. Part of this discomfort is around sharing my own vulnerabilities. As Brené Brown says, "vulnerability is strength, not weakness." So, as you can see, the stories I have shared with you have shaped me immeasurably.

I have written a great deal about Q's mental illness, but not about his life as a double amputee. His losing his legs and his life in a wheelchair gave me a greater awareness and understanding of physical disabilities, and I watch the wheelchair tennis at the Australian Open with a deep appreciation of the skill involved, particularly the movement around the court and how difficult this is while trying to hit the ball. Beyond the sporting arena, I notice things in daily life that I would not have seen before. We used to go out to restaurants for dinner as a family for birthdays and other celebrations, and we would always need to think if the venue was appropriate for Q. He would need an easily accessible space at the table without a chair, easy to get in and out of, and without much through traffic behind him. We had to consider steps too. Ideally the restaurant needed a ramp and no steps at all, and Q had to be able to get in and out of the toilet with his wheelchair. When he wanted to go for a swim at the beach, we had to find somewhere where he could get his wheelchair close to the water, and then he would crawl in on his hands and knees. This didn't look very elegant, but it was inevitable. I knew that crawling on his hands and knees was humiliating, but it was the only way to get to certain places and over bumpy terrain. Even going for a swim at the local pool was a challenge. He had to get into the pool after wheeling as close to the edge as he could and learnt to use his strong arms to manoeuvre himself into the pool as well as getting in and out of my car whenever I took him out, but as he got older and heavier, it became more difficult for him.

Prior to Q's 'accident' I didn't even notice these issues for people with a disability. I had no concept of what life must be like for people in a wheelchair. Now I see it daily, and in addition I am mindful of the complex overlap between mental and physical disabilities. Our health systems are seldom equipped to cope with both. It is typically a divided world where clinicians have been educated to help patients who fit neatly into either one of these categories, but more needs to be done to train people to deal with both physical and mental challenges.

I have written about my father's bipolar disorder and his alcoholism, but worst for me was his inability to show love or affection. One of the greatest needs we all have as human beings is to feel loved and accepted. We all want to belong and connect, and to know that we are valued, and the greatest joys and most bitter disappointments involve relationships. From the time we are born, our most urgent need is to for both our parents to show that they love us unconditionally. I realise now that Dad did love me, but for most of my life I did not know it. As a result, I felt inferior, humiliated, ashamed of who I was, and, compared to my incredibly intelligent father, dumb and stupid. I just wanted Dad's approval.

My level of self-worth was very low as a child. Without knowing it at the time, I did many things for approval, and to be loved and accepted. I think tennis was a part of this - something I was good at from when I was very young. I received the attention I sought and was recognised and rewarded. I came first in many sports and that felt good. Even now, when I go back to my school reunions (I'm about to attend the 40th year anniversary of my Year 12 this weekend), one of the first questions old mates ask is "Do you still play tennis?" It feels good to be remembered for something you did well. I first identified my own strong need for approval in my late twenties as I began working as an Organisational Psychologist, and it took many years to minimise it and do things for other reasons such as achievement rather than approval. I'm still working on this in my late fifties, and I still do things for approval, but I'm certainly more mindful of this now.

The other influence my father has had on me relates to parenting. For a long time, I wanted to be the opposite of Dad, and to be a different father to the one I had. I was desperate to be a great dad, affectionate and loving. I wanted my children to know that I love them unconditionally. They are 18, 21 and 23 years of age now, and I know that they realise how much I love them. I am still doing my very best to be the father that my father was not able to be for me. This may sound as though I disapprove of my father, but I do understand that he did the best he could. I am not blaming him. He did not intend to have this impact on me. It was something he was not conscious of and yet it had this effect on my life. I also see this in my daily interactions. I am a hugger. I hug many of my mates instead of giving them a handshake. I like to give and receive physical affection as well as words of appreciation. I know this all stems from my relationship with Dad.

How has this shaped me personally and professionally?

Mum and Dad's divorce has made me reflect deeply on my relationship with my wife Lynne. Next month we will celebrate our 30th wedding anniversary, three more years than my parents were together. What have I learnt from their mistakes?

I have found that relationships are about learning. I am not the same person that I was 30 years ago. I have grown, developed, and evolved. Lynne is not the same person either. For me a key question is, as you both change over 30 years, can you both adapt and grow together? Or do you grow apart? Do you understand what your partner needs from you to be happy? Can you adjust to the fact that what may have made them happy 15 years ago is no longer making them happy?

In the early stages of a relationship, love and physical attraction seem to be a major factor in a couple's happiness, but after many years together they need more than this. They need to like each other and not just love each other. They need to like spending a lot of time together and get a lot of joy out of it. They need to respect each other's differences. Often couples in a relationship are different, and in fact frequently they have opposite thinking preferences and personality styles. This can be a strength and help them to parent and to run a home. However, both partners must respect and value these differences, rather than wishing the other person were more like them. Once this respect for difference is lost, it puts a strain on the relationship. I have understood this for a long time, and attempted to respect and value the different qualities both Lynne and I bring to the relationship and to the way we bring up our children.

I have also realised that it is not just the divorce that affected us children, it was the nature of the divorce and the surrounding hostility that made it more difficult to deal with. I have sometimes thought that if a couple stays together purely for the sake of the children but argue all the time and do not demonstrate to their children what a good relationship looks like, it is probably more helpful for the children that they separate.

It is by staying together and learning, developing and evolving together that your children can observe a healthy, positive relationship. I aspire not just to be a good dad, but also to be a good parent together with Lynne. Whilst we haven't always got it right over 30 years, I am proud of the journey so far and I believe the children have benefitted from this approach as they grow into delightful young adults.

I have wondered about the impact of Dad's drinking on me, and some of the drugs Q used such as marijuana. I think both have affected me. As long as I can recall, Dad always had a little 'pot gut'. I asked him about it one day, and he told me he had had it since he was about 27 years old and had never quite been able to lose it. He said that he had started drinking quite a bit then, and this was initially responsible for his change in body. I remember thinking to myself that I didn't want to get a pot gut like Dad, particularly because I didn't think I could get rid of it again, and that was the motivation for me to lead a healthy life and develop the healthy daily habits that I have maintained for most of my adult life. Apart from two years when I stopped drinking alcohol completely, I have drunk a little regularly, but usually only drink, and I am a social drinker rather than drinking at home daily. I think these habits have most likely been influenced by watching my father.

A greater influence on me and my children has been marijuana. I have told them about their significantly increased risk of an adverse reaction to smoking marijuana, and that the evidence shows that schizophrenia runs in families. The best estimates of the hereditability of schizophrenia are that 70-80% are associated with genetics, and cannabis use may be a contributing factor in the development of schizophrenia, particularly for those already at risk. Its use doubles the rate of contracting the disease. In the environment that our children grow up in, it is likely that they will be exposed to many different types of drugs, both legal and illegal. The one drug whose serious risks to their mental health I have been extremely keen to ensure that they are aware of is cannabis. As well as the data being very strong and clear on this, I have obviously been influenced by my personal experiences with Q.

Observing Glenn's life and then retelling his and Yvette's story again in this book has caused me to feel a range of emotions, mostly extreme sadness at the trauma and pain he suffered and the impact on my sister and their three children. I have also felt despair and helplessness. Glenn tried almost everything to get better. Treatments that usually work simply failed to help, and the only thing he couldn't do was fail in what he believed were his duty and obligation to work in the family business. He had such a strong sense of loyalty to the business his father began, and his brother Gary continued and successfully grew, and this quirk made him stay well beyond a time that made sense for his health. I was disappointed when he made the decision to return after Gary asked him to. I was disappointed because I had seen a massive improvement in his behaviour and mood when he stopped working there, and I knew he would deteriorate again once he went back. This turned out to be correct, unfortunately. I also felt upset and angry that this was a choice he and Gary made. It was a poor decision, and Glenn suffered greatly as a result.

I am very close to my sister Yvette. We have been through a lot together and that has brought us even closer than perhaps might have been the case otherwise. I have wanted to help her and her children throughout this ordeal and done what I could to make a positive difference by being available to listen and support them in whatever ways I can. Glenn's tragedy has motivated me to reach out and proactively build deeper connections with my nephew and two nieces. I love them almost as if they were my children and am grateful to have built a stronger bond through sharing this tragedy.

How have these experiences informed my work?

―

With the wonderful quote from Danish philosopher Soren Kierkegaard "life must be lived going forward but can only be understood looking backwards" in mind, it is fascinating to look back at my choices in psychology and realise how my life has shaped my work. I began as a sport psychologist, and my passion for this type of work came directly from my own personal experience trying to make it as a professional tennis player and realising that I did not have all the mental tools I needed to cope with the pressure, stress, and anxiety involved in elite-level sport. Back then in the '80s, it was thought that you were either born with the mental strength or not, but now we know that you can learn most of the skills needed to become psychologically strong and not just physically able.

There was not quite enough work in the field of Sport Psychology for me to make a reasonable living, so I supplemented the work with drug and alcohol counselling for approximately five years, and I also did some work with patients with mental illness. I understood the things that gave me energy and those that drained me and realised that I gained energy from the positive aspects of Sport Psychology. Essentially, I was taking normal to high-functioning people and helping them do better.

With respect to the drug and alcohol counselling work, I felt that I was working with people who were struggling in life, and I was only able to help them survive but not to thrive. Regarding the work with people with mental illness, it simply felt too close to home and drained me. It meant I didn't have enough energy to give to Q and Craig. This led me to change careers and become an Organisational Psychologist way back in 1996, when I successfully completed a Master of Organisational Psychology degree at Monash University in Melbourne. My thinking behind this decision was that I wanted to use positive psychology principles to help normal people reach their full potential and find ways of thriving and flourishing, but to have enough energy left to help my family because I understood that it would be a long hard struggle for Q and Craig. I wanted to be emotionally available for them and for my broader family.

Over the last 28 years of working as an organisational psychologist, I have operated across almost all the main areas of this profession and, without planning it, for the last ten years or so I have developed a passion for and expertise in the overlap between leadership and wellbeing. The leadership aspect of the work I do is closely linked to performance, and I have learnt that the greatest positive impact you can contribute to an organisation is to help the leaders to lead better. This can drive long-term business success. My desire for high performance is no doubt influenced by my sporting career and a strong competitive drive. So, I have come full circle back to mental health and wellbeing. Without a concrete plan, I have been naturally drawn to focus this latter part of my work on both leadership and wellbeing, which of course makes total sense. Furthermore, because I have a high drive for achievement, through combining my interests in all forms of wellbeing with leadership development, I am able to maximise my impact, positively influencing hundreds or even thousands of people through the leadership and wellbeing work I do, whereas if I were to work as a clinical psychologist I would only be touching people at an individual level. I prefer making a profound difference to the lives of many people.

Beyond the nature of what I do now, my experiences have influenced and shaped the way I work and my belief systems. I believe that we should all aim to bring our authentic self to work, and that it is necessary to work with and help the whole person and not just the work person. Since COVID, many others share this belief, however for years leaders in business thought that you should separate home from work. I don't agree. Leaders should be authentic in the way they lead.

Their lives at home do have a significant influence on the way they lead their team members, and I don't think it is possible to separate them. I do believe that you need to switch off and psychologically detach from work when you are at home, but that is different to being real, human, authentic, and genuine when you are at work. This is a big part of who I am. My research in psychology has helped me understand why people do things, and my specific study of organisational psychology has given me a much broader systems view of the environment we operate in. I am now able to step back from individual examples and stories like my own and reflect on the society we live in and how it affects us all. My aim now is to balance the evidence-based research and my lived experience to ensure I have a level of authenticity and look for practical solutions to the many complex challenges facing us all. Furthermore, I enjoy engaging with leaders and people more fully using storytelling. This helps to build trust and connection and enables me to demonstrate compassion and real understanding and not just text-book consulting, which is important.

How has this shaped the people around me?

Mum

Q and Craig have been an ongoing worry for Mum, although Craig was more challenging from an early age and caused her a great deal of anxiety, whereas Q was much less of a day-to-day problem as a child, except he couldn't keep still. Mum was concerned about the influence Craig had on us children. He was very aggressive and strong, particularly as a teenager, and he used to bully and hit us. As a mother, she was torn between Craig and her other three children, and she used to try desperately to find someone to help Craig with his schoolwork. He suffered from debilitating headaches because he could not handle school, and towards the end of Year 10, they called Mum and told her Craig should leave before the end of the year and get a job. Mum was upset, and worried that if Craig could not cope at school, he would struggle to cope with life afterwards.

After Q's 'nervous breakdown' and diagnosis with schizophrenia, Mum's life was never the same, and it all contributed to her high blood pressure. But, notwithstanding, in a way I think her own upbringing helped her with Q and Craig. Mum's father believed in Communism and Marxism, and Mum was raised to take care of those less fortunate, to share what she had, not to be greedy, to help people in need, etc. Q gave Mum a cause to focus on, and she joined the local Parents and Friends Support Group for people with schizophrenia where she was

President for 12 years, committed to helping others in a similar plight. In her later years, this all became too emotionally draining for her, and she gradually let go as the baton passed to Yvette and me to look after Q. However, Mum couldn't do nothing, and she then took up the worthy cause of helping refugees. It is in her blood.

Craig was always more difficult to help for several reasons. There was no clear diagnosis of his problems until later in life, and so it was difficult to work out how to help and what to do. He was less likeable as a young person than Q, who was amusing, personable and just more fun to be around. Craig was angry and talked about himself constantly, but he has changed. He has grown up and developed and understands now, and, at 60, has a lot to be proud of. He is no longer self-centred and angry. He is still anxious at times, but rarely angry. He is grateful for any help, and listens, and asks sensible questions. He laughs a lot and is good to be with. Mum notices this and looks for ways to support him although she is 86.

Mum is very strong, partly because she has had to be strong but also because this is in her makeup and her upbringing. She has never felt the need to cry on people's shoulders. Her best friend for over 30 years is Judith Rafferty, and she and Mum are very considerate and supportive of each other. They were both foundation members of the Parents and Friends Support Group, and Mum has found comfort with other parents who have had similar difficulties raising children with various forms of mental illness and feels that talking about it with people who understand is quite a cathartic experience. She once told me "You can say what you like to us, we are practically unshockable."

Mum has always said that anything that helps the sufferer, helps the carer. She has fought as hard as she could for her entire life as a parent to get the best possible treatment for Q and Craig. Margaret Leggett, the previous President of World Schizophrenia, said to Mum once "People with a mental illness; it's like the umbilical cord was never broken."

Mum believes you must work at having a balanced life. Many parents of children with mental illness devote their entire lives to mentally unwell children, and they get worn out over the years without achieving much. Mum is sure you can't help others without taking care of yourself along the way. She has spoken to many parents who don't think they have done enough, and she used to think the same but now asks where you draw the line. I tell her that she has done enough. She has done her very best for her entire life.

Yvette

Yvette has been shaped and affected by the events outlined in this book possibly the most out of all of us. She was always sensitive and empathetic; however, the last 35 years have brought out even stronger emotions. As a child Yvette suffered from terrible eczema all over her body. She used to scratch it in her sleep at night and wake up with bloodstains on her pillow and sheets. She had a lovely friend, Michelle, who used to come to our place regularly to play and would apply soothing creams. However, not all children were so nice, and Yvette was teased badly and called "rashy" and "rashbash". As a result, she has raised her children not to tease people about anything physically wrong with them, and through her experiences of mental illness she has extended this to not being judgemental. For example, if they see a homeless person or a drug addict on the street, they should not judge them, but rather understand that there is most likely a trauma and/or mental illness involved. She has taught them to be grateful for a mind that works reasonably well, and glad to be able to think clearly and function at a normal level. Yvette is an endlessly kind, caring, and compassionate human being.

However, mental illness has frequently interrupted her life. Whenever a crisis has occurred, Yvette has had to leave her children alone and race off to help sort out whatever tragic event was unfolding. This has led to her feeling constantly on edge, and her anxiety is usually triggered by little things. She works hard to stay positive but tries to prepare herself for the worst. The many phone calls with bad news she has received have contributed to a sense of impending doom, which she has suffered from for many years. She fears that the worst will happen, because the worst has happened to her repeatedly. Many people have told her that she is strong, and the way she copes is amazing, but she doesn't feel amazing, and the people who are close to her know that she has had many of her own struggles. She has taken anti-depressant medication for a long time now and is fully aware of a couple of vices that help her cope, including alcohol. She drinks too much, and understands it is not helpful, but for a short period it helps grief to recede into the background.

When Yvette was a teenager, Craig embarrassed her. He had some unusual friends, and she recalls a somewhat traumatic occasion when she was about 13 years old and had a friend over. A friend of Craig's grabbed Yvette's friend by the ankles and held her upside down, then proceeded to put ice down her tube skirt. As a teenager, Craig was quite difficult to deal with, but he no longer embarrasses her, and although he still doesn't seem to understand social norms or cues to behaviours that are considered normal, Yvette has learnt not to care what other people think, and just says to herself "He is my brother, and I love him; he is the way he is." She accepts Craig exactly as he is and believes if people judge him negatively that is their loss, and perhaps they have been lucky enough not to have had some of the terrible experiences we have and so they don't understand. When helping Craig with banking or medical appointments for example, he will be inappropriately lewd and make silly jokes, but in the end, he has everyone laughing and people warm to him.

A teenager when Mum and Dad separated, Yvette longed for Dad's love and affection. She has several girlfriends who are close to their fathers, but although Yvette never was, when she was 22, she worked with Dad as a Judge's Associate in the County Court and was able to see firsthand what a brilliant mind he had, and how he could make big, important decisions quickly and sensibly. This helped her understand and accept his inadequate emotional side and to value his keen intellect. In his last few years, suffering from old age dementia, he changed and softened, and even told her he loved her.

Reflecting on her marriage with Glenn and the fact that she was the one who ended it, Yvette felt she had to do that because her life had got to a stage of sink or swim. She had been suffering for years and was drowning as Glenn dragged her down with him. She still loved him but needed to save herself. She will never get over the fact that it reached the point where she felt she had no other option, but they did stay very close after they separated, and Yvette was keen to ensure that their children spent as much time with their father as possible, even though at times he did not take care of them very well - not through lack of love or care, but just because he was so depressed. One of her best friends, Heather, once asked "Do you think you should pull the pin and not send the kids to Glenn?" referring to the fact that Glenn was not looking after them. Yvette said, "They need time with their dad, even if he doesn't do much with them." They were not in danger, even though he did not really supervise them.

When she was six years old, Georgia was with Glenn for the weekend, and she fell and broke her arm running on the grass watching Tim play football. Glenn took her to hospital and called Yvette. While

Yvette listened to the nurse ask Georgia questions because she had to have surgery, when Georgia was asked what she had had to eat she responded "Shapes. Leftover muffins." She had not eaten breakfast, nor a proper lunch, and that was all she had had all day. She wasn't in danger, yet neither was she properly cared for.

Despite all this, Yvette still feels guilty about leaving Glenn, and can't help wondering whether that brought on his decision to take his life. This gnaws at her regularly, and Glenn's suicide has caused her to grieve four times over, because she grieves for herself and for each of her three children. She grieves for the man she loved so much, and for the breakdown of their marriage, and feels very alone as a parent financially, physically, and emotionally, especially at times when a father would usually be there. Happy moments with her children are tinged with sadness because he is not there. When her two elder children had their 21st birthday parties, Glenn was not there to give a speech, and when the kids bought their first cars there was no one to teach them how to put petrol in, check the oil and water, and put air in the tyres.

Yvette' experiences with the four men closest to her, Glenn, Q, Craig, and Dad, who all had mental health issues, have made her outspoken about mental illness. When Glenn began going downhill, he didn't want Yvette to tell anyone because of the stigma. However, eventually Yvette said, "I need to tell people because it is affecting my life and the kids."

Glenn's tragedy and suicide have obviously altered Yvette's social life. When his suicide is mentioned in casual conversations she ends up in tears, which embarrasses her. She used to be the life of the party, but now she feels that she has lost her spark. She also believes that she has become too empathetic and cannot regulate her emotions. Would she have been like this anyway? Have these events made her more emotional?

Yvette has learnt many lessons from her experiences with mental illness and suicide. She fully understands that life is short, and we all need to make the most of it, and she knows that she needs to appreciate what she has, especially her many wonderful friends and family. She sees who her friends are in times of need. Several good friends helped in small but important ways in the weeks after Glenn passed away. Some cooked for her, and others did her shopping. Yvette was so engulfed with grief that she was not even able to drive for some time after Glenn's death, and friends took her children to their sports activities. She feels it is incredibly important to tell people you love them... assuming you do!

I asked Yvette if she had a magic wand that could fix our mental health system, what she would do. She would "ensure people are more aware of mental illness and exactly what it means, and how it affects a person and takes away their control over their life and many of their actions." She wishes people could be more compassionate and helpful. When Q first became mentally unwell, his friends gradually dropped him. It was just too hard for them, and we should be able to do better than this as a society.

Seeing the mental health system up close for over three decades, Yvette knows it has a lot of flaws and needs improvement. For example, there should be an emergency entrance to hospital psychiatric wards. A normal emergency ward is not the place for a psychotic patient. It's not fair on the staff, other patients, their families, and the patients themselves. These issues need to be improved. Yvette understands that mental health professionals have a hard job, but many of them don't listen to the family's cries for help or take them seriously enough. This angers and frustrates her, despite the many wonderfully positive aspects to our mental health system.

Tim
(Yvette's eldest son who is now 26)

When Tim reflected on his father, he stated, "I never remember him being 100 percent well mentally. You would see bits and pieces of him. He would be on and off, either crashed out and not able to do anything or highly productive and building things."

Tim shared that Glenn was "very smart and he could do anything he put his mind to, but he struggled with the stress of things." He would get anxiety from pressure. Tim read letters from when Glenn was in his early 20's where he shared that he was feeling pressure and anxiety when he was a foreman in charge of about 20 men on a building site in Melbourne". Glenn knew something was wrong with him. However, the stigma around anxiety and mental health issues meant he didn't talk about it, and he couldn't fully acknowledge it to himself or others. Tim is now a carpenter, working in the building industry. Tim suggested this industry is probably worse than other industries for men's health because it is very masculine and not normal to talk about mental health issues such as anxiety. In the building industry, as a man "you must be mentally strong".

"Dad was better when I was young, but I saw less of him because he worked such long hours". As he got older Glenn had freedom to work less hours, but he was not doing better mentally. Glenn felt guilty about letting the family down. He never wanted to be there. He didn't feel like it was his business and was not motivated to build it up like his brother. Glenn felt pressured. Tim tried to go to the yard at work to be around him more. Around the age of 12 Tim began riding his bike to the yard after school. Tim recalls, "at work I felt the tension for dad. He told me he hated it, but he got it done." Tim has learnt to pick up on emotions and believes he is now hyper-sensitive to other's feelings.

Yvette and Glenn separated when Tim was in Year 7 at school. Tim thought his entire world was crashing down. "I knew something big was happening, but it was out of my control." Tim struggled to remember them together. He has more memories after they separated. He saw a lot more of his father after they divorced. When Glenn was well, they spent a lot of time together. Tim was racing motorbikes and Glenn supported him by taking him to the local motocross track and to many races that were a long way from home. He feels lucky to have spent this time with his dad however, Glenn didn't share a lot with Tim. "He wouldn't tell me to the extent that he was totally honest. I don't know how dark his mind went."

As he spiralled down, Glenn wasn't well enough to look after Tim, but he didn't need looking after. Tim was 18 years old, and he went to stay with his dad because he wanted to see him. Tim ended up doing things on his own because with his father it was "hit and miss". Glenn was often in bed or watching television. Tim ended up being the parent. It forced Tim to grow up quickly. Tim had a long-term girlfriend Emi, and they spent considerable time together. Later Tim felt guilty about this because he could have spent more time with his dad.

In the weeks leading up to Glenn taking his own life, Tim shared that "it was scary as dad went downhill". He could see that his father was very unwell, and it was confusing for Tim. He had seen him improve previously so there was still a small amount of hope and yet he felt helpless, and yet he was running out of hope.

On the day Glenn took his own life, Tim recalls that he was at trade school building some stairs. At the time, he felt good about what he was doing with his life. He came home to be told the tragic news by Yvette. After the shock, he wondered if he could have done more. For a while he felt guilty but after years of therapy Tim has been able to work through this emotion and is no longer feeling guilty.

Tim saw a psychologist for about 5 years. He felt that it was good to talk to someone who was independent. Initially the sessions were every 4-6 weeks and then every few months. He reflected that "after a while the sessions stopped being about dad and started being about me and my future". The sessions were particularly helpful for Tim. He felt he had someone to talk to and he felt comfortable with his psychologist.

Now as a 26-year-old, he feels wiser, sharing with me that "it is like I have lived through a few different lives. I think more deeply about things in life." Tim values things differently to many others. For example, "people put money at the top of their list whereas my mental health and fitness are at the top of my list, and I like to have a good group of people around me". He has decided that if people around him are not a good influence, he simply cuts them out of his close friendship circle. He consciously surrounds himself with "good people".

Tim stated that "people whinge and complain about things, and they don't have perspective." Tim has done a lot of self-reflection. He has listened to a lot of podcasts and learnt a great deal. After his relationship with Emi ended, Tim went out with Jess (who was studying to be a psychologist). Jess was great for Tim, and this helped Tim talk through his challenges.

Tim and Jess split up about 18 months ago, after living together for a while. Tim decided to pack up and travel on his own around Australia. He consciously chose this path as he realised it would force him to get out of his comfort zone. He was looking for the next thing. He needed time to heal and to reset. After an incredible 12 months travelling around the country, he has now settled in Cairns (nearly 3,000 kilometres from him hometown of Melbourne) for the last 4 months. He made a lot of connections to people in different places. It taught him that you don't have to be stuck in life. Tim now feels that he has choices in life.

He watched his father get trapped and Tim has done the opposite. He is happy now. "Everything is going well. I'm settled in one place. I have met lots of good people. Cairns is a lovely area to live in." Tim further shared that he also doesn't feel trapped in Cairns, and he could leave if he wanted to. He is choosing to be in Cairns and is not forced to do it.

In terms of the future, Tim has always wanted to run his own business, but he has seen the positive and negative side of this. He doesn't want to be drowning in work and burnt out like his father. He wants to try to balance out work and life as much as possible.

Jess
(Yvette's oldest daughter who is currently 24 years old)

Jess feels she had to grow up a lot faster than her peers. Georgia was only five or six when her parents separated, and when the children stayed with Glenn, Jess had to look after Georgia most of the time.

Her experience with her father has made her more resilient, and Jess understands more about people and their struggles. Like Yvette, she said, "I don't' sweat the small stuff", and "People complain about little things in life, and I think really, there is so much more…" Jess has developed enough courage to call people out on some things, and when people joke about killing themselves, she challenges them, given her father did take his own life.

Jess recalls going to many events with her mother, but Glenn was never there because he wasn't well. She would tell her friends "My daddy is sick, but not the normal sick… he will never get better…" She once wrote in a letter "He goes into hospital, but it is not a normal sick, he is sick in the head. It makes him sad." In high school Jess was able to tell friends that her dad had depression. "He is really sad and can't get out of bed," and most of her friends responded well.

Seeing her friends do things with their own fathers was upsetting for Jess at the time, but now it is even worse because she knows she will never get him back. When Yvette and Glenn got divorced, Jess felt unutterable sadness. She told me about when they first separated and sat the children down together to tell them. When they said, "Mummy and Daddy still love each other very much, but we are not in love anymore," Jess just wept. With respect to her father's suicide, she feels sorrow but no guilt, and fewer moments trigger her grief.

All this helps her to be more aware of people's feelings, more conscious of their needs. Like her mother, she is extremely empathetic and understanding, particularly with people with disabilities.

Georgia
(Yvette's youngest daughter who is currently 19 years old)

Some aspects of Georgia's life have been affected similarly and others differently. Since she is much younger, she can't recall Glenn being a father figure. She felt that Jess was her parent when they were staying with Glenn, and barely remembers him living in their family home or Yvette and Glenn being together. He moved out when Georgia was six or seven and was in hospital for a lot of her childhood. Scheduled times to see him were often cancelled because he was too unwell, although the children usually stayed with him every second weekend and on Wednesdays. She recalls that "Dad wouldn't put me to sleep." Dinner would be an easy meal, or Jess, who was only 11 or 12, made it, and then she would put Georgia to bed. Georgia said "Dad would watch TV; he wouldn't make sure we went to bed. It would be about 11pm on a school night, and he wouldn't say go to bed." So, Georgia went to bed whenever she wanted or when Jess suggested it. The following morning, she would usually wake Glenn up and ask him to drive her to school. Although it was quite a long walk of about 30 minutes and she was about nine years old, Glenn would frequently say "I'm not up to it, you'll have to walk." In the mornings, Jess did her hair, and on one occasion she said to Georgia "You will regret doing a side ponytail," and Georgia, clearly understanding the fashions of the time, responded "What do you mean? It's in!"

Georgia reflects that "for most of my life, I got the worst of his illness, so I didn't see a decline. I didn't know his behaviour was not normal until I went to other people's homes and realised." Georgia also says that she became more independent as a result. She used to either buy lunch on Thursdays when she stayed with Glenn or she would make it herself, usually a Nutella sandwich. She told me that she had anger issues and tantrums until she was about 10 or 11 years old, and lots of built-up stress. At home she did not know how to control her feelings, although at school she never showed her anger.

She remembers getting angry over little things. In Glenn's suicide note, he wrote "I love my kids", but he didn't say "I love Georgia", which upset her, and she also resents that Jess, and their brother Tim were old enough to have had a life with Glenn.

Notwithstanding this, Georgia saw her parents' divorce as positive. She can't recall Glenn living at home, and her memories start a long time after their separation. Georgia noticed that her friends whose parents were divorced used to argue, but she said, "Dad would come over and stay for an hour while he and Mum chatted," and "Mum was a single mother, but this was behind closed doors; she did everything with no help from Dad. No one else understood that, but once they separated it was out in the open."

Two years after Glenn's death, when Georgia was 13 during lock down, she said "Mum sent the coroner's report to me. Maybe it wasn't suicide?" She simply didn't want that to be the truth.

Five years after Glenn died, Q's death triggered a lot for Georgia. The service for Q was held in the same chapel, and Q was her next closest relative to die. She was 16… old enough to understand death a little better.

Georgia saw a psychologist and a psychiatrist and started medication for bipolar disorder two weeks later. Whilst it has been a heroic struggle for her, I'm pleased and proud to say that she is working through it all, seeking help, talking openly, and demonstrating outstanding courage. She is naturally drawn to people who have been through trauma – "we get each other, they understand," she says. She too has become more compassionate and understanding of mental illness.

What have I learnt from these experiences? What has helped me?

Family

I have learnt a great deal over the last 37 years and come to realise the crucial role that our families play in helping us all to cope. In many ways, our shared struggles, challenges and suffering have enhanced our bond with each other. This helps everyone in both good times and bad. We are not a perfect family – I'm talking about my siblings and my mother at this point, and not my wife and three children. We argue, and sometimes even yell at each other. We disagree, and we are loud when we get together. However, regardless of how crazy we must sometimes seem to other people, we care about each other and have made many sacrifices over the years to help each other out. Our love for each other is unconditional. This is such a critical part of helping me to cope. I have got to add that my immediate family, my wife Lynne and our three children, have all been an incredible support to me. While they have not usually been directly involved in providing care for Q or Craig, just knowing that they understand and provide the environment that enables me to prioritise support for my brothers has been invaluable. They also demonstrate to me constantly that they care, and they show compassion.

Friends

The support of close friends is also key to not only surviving but to finding ways to thrive. I am fortunate to have amazing mates whom I can talk to. I don't want to mention their names, but I do feel that, while you don't need to have a large group of people, you do have to have a couple of close friends to talk you through whatever is going on. I have had great support from mates who just listen to me without necessarily giving advice unless I ask for it. They usually help by being non-judgemental, non-inflammatory (that is they don't make it worse than it needs to be, and they find a way to help me by talking things through calmly), and available when I need them.

Mindset

Another factor that has helped me is my mindset. I practise feeling gratitude each day. Each night just before I go to sleep, I make myself go through a list of all the little things that have happened during the day that I am grateful for. They can be as small as a lovely cup of coffee in the morning, or someone who did something nice for me or said thank you for something I had done. Nothing major, but the daily habit of pausing and recognising that there are many things in my life that I should appreciate, particularly when I stop and compare the quality of my life with Q, Craig, and Glenn's lives. I immediately feel lucky and profoundly grateful, and any problems I have seem to shrink. It doesn't mean my issues are not real, but it helps to put them in perspective.

Helping others

I have also found that when I help other people, particularly Q and Craig but also in the latter part of Dad's life, it helps me. When I can pause and stop my busy life and take time out to focus my energy on helping them, it makes me happier. It increases my sense of purpose and meaning, helps me to feel more fulfilled, and gives me a sense of belonging. By focusing on helping other people, my own problems melt into the background, and I feel more joy.

Some tools

As a psychologist, I have learnt many helpful frameworks and tools. One of the most useful in this context is known as the Circle of Control or Circle of Concern. Essentially it is a model that helps you to control what you can and let go of things outside of your control. This is easier said than done. Often when dealing with family members who have mental health issues, there are many things that you are concerned about but have no control over. It has been very important for me to consciously let go of as much as I can and focus on all the things I can control, and work on acting on those. In the middle of this are some things you can influence but not directly control. I ask myself "What can I influence? And what do I need to let go of?" Inevitably it boils down to the fact that I can only control my own response to a situation, and I can control how I seek to influence others but must deliberately let go of my need to control outcomes. This is not always easy to do, but it is a great framework to use. It also helps to ensure I do not overly personalise events. I do not own elements of this story that are not mine to own. I must not feel guilty for things I could not control. I have learnt to tell myself that I have done my best in this situation, and I could not have done any more, and that's OK.

Taking care of my own wellbeing

The final point I want to make about what has helped me to be resilient and cope with the challenges of the last 37 years is the importance I have placed on my own wellbeing. I focus on physical, mental, and social wellbeing. The answer to physical wellbeing includes exercise, diet, hydration, rest, and sleep. The connection between our physical and mental health has been well documented. I know that when I am feeling physically strong and healthy, I am more likely to also feel mentally and emotionally well. I exercise almost every day and have done so for most of my life, and I believe it is critical to keep moving and be active, although as I get older, I have had to modify the specific exercises I do to cope with my aging body. Without being ridiculous about it, I also ensure I eat well and focus on food that provides me with sustainable energy. I have not always drunk enough water, but this is something that I am mindful of and an important part of physical health. Rest and sleep are also essential. I aim to get a good night's sleep, and I usually do. I am a good sleeper, and I believe in building a healthy bedtime routine. I try to go to bed at the same time each night, and to get up at the same time, or at least within 30 minutes of my usual routine so that my body has built a regular sleeping and waking habit. All this has certainly helped me.

For mental wellbeing, I focus on my mindset and on what is in my control. I also try to understand the connection between my thoughts and emotions. I usually find that my emotions are preceded by thoughts, and when I feel negative it is usually because I have unhelpful thoughts. Then I take time to pause and reflect, and to either change my thinking or find a way to let go of the unhelpful thoughts.

Social wellbeing is also important to me, an area not discussed enough in my view. One of the most important things that drives happiness and health is to have a few friends whom you know well, and trust and love - close friends whom you can talk to about anything, who have your back, and whom you can call upon. You must work at this. It doesn't just happen. As I have aged, I have realised that my circle of friends diminishes, and I have taken time to reach out to friends so that I don't lose touch or take them for granted. This doesn't mean I need a lot of friends - just a few good ones.

What else should we do as a society?

As a society in an Australian context, we need to continually review and improve our mental health systems and to amend our conversations at a social and cultural level. The entry point for getting emergency help needs to change drastically. While I agree that people with mental illnesses should be living in the community with the appropriate level of support, when people like Q must go to hospital, the system is inadequately prepared. As a reasonably sophisticated society, we can and should do better. A psychologically ill patient should not have to go to a physical emergency area and wait for hours overnight next to physically unwell patients for a hospital bed as happened to us on many occasions when Q was delusional. He should not have been in the emergency ward with people with physical health problems. My mother has advocated for some time for separate emergency wards for physical and psychological issues. Hospitals should find a way to cater for these different needs, although I understand that hospital beds are scarce, and this is an exceptionally difficult problem to manage from a financial perspective. But the government must do more to ensure there are an appropriate number of beds to cope with the demand and need to keep mentally unwell people safe from the harm they may do to themselves or others when they are calling out for help.

The police and ambulance services are often at the forefront of these emergencies and crises, although we have come a long way since the days of putting people like Q in a straitjacket. They are now trained to manage patients with a severe mental illness, but I believe a lot more can be done, in particular training and education for first responders should be more thorough, so that they can react appropriately.

Our services should also integrate better. The Crisis Assessment and Treatment Team (CATT) has been established for years and has helped our family, yet it could still be improved. The staff are frequently not well trained, and the decision by one of the CATT workers not to help Yvette when Q was having a terrible episode, and just sending her to emergency at Monash Hospital in the middle of the night was wrong. Is this a training issue? Is it just an issue for this worker? How do CATT team members work with the hospital, police, and ambulance services in this situation? It didn't work for Yvette and Q on that occasion, nor on other occasions. Furthermore, the CATT team were often not available when we needed them as they are understaffed and under-resourced. It is nice to know we have a system to help with crises, however the entire system needs overhauling.

Better integration of therapies to help those with mental illness would make a marked difference. Q had a case manager for many years from the Clayton Mobile Support and Treatment Service (MSTS), and later from the Clayton Continuing Care Team (CCT). The CCT provides case management support and ongoing mental health follow-up and relapse prevention, whereas the MSTS offers intensive day-to-day case management support. These services are great in many ways, but still fail to adequately support people like Q. They aspire to integrate services, and they often get it right, but not often enough. Q had a very caring case manager called Florence, who knew and understood him well. She even came to his funeral. However, their services are only available from 8:30am to 5pm. The MSTS is designed for people with severe mental health issues and their episodes usually happen after 5pm. Whom do we turn to at these times? We would usually call the CATT team but they frequently didn't understand the context and so we would just turn up at emergency and go through the whole scenario again of waiting for hours in the middle of the night with a series of doctors who didn't know Q and didn't know that we had done this many times over the years. They didn't know the history.

Other examples of a lack of integration of services relate to the people providing medication, and counselling and support groups being completely independent of each other. Q had a psychiatrist who looked after his medication, an ongoing challenge, particularly adjusting it based on the severity of his symptoms and the side effects. Q also had compliance issues and there were frequent periods when he didn't take his medication. He had opportunities to join various support groups, and the one that stands out is the support group at the Malvern Clinic way back in the '80s and '90s, when unfortunately, it was closed. I remember protesting in the streets about that, because it provided Q with fabulous support. He enjoyed going there, and when it was not replaced with anything nearly as good, he lost something that had really improved the quality of his life. Another group he loved over the last decade or so was his art group at Dixon House. He would attend regularly, sit with other people, and create his masterpieces.

The only therapy Q ever had was when Mum took him to Hearing Voices sessions that were organised by the Mental Awareness Group in South Yarra. He attended weekly one-hour, one-on-one counselling sessions about six times. Some people respond well; however, they did not seem to make any difference to Q.

The above examples of services Q received in relation to his medication, his counselling needs, and support groups show that their lack of integration diminishes their benefit, because when offered in isolation they fail to treat the person in a holistic manner, resulting in overall reduced effectiveness.

Having conversations

I believe that the first thing we should change as a society is the conversations we have about mental illness. We need to learn to be more comfortable with our vulnerabilities. Sometimes life is hard, and people suffer; we need to understand that this is normal. Sometimes life is not fair or easy, and that's OK. It is sometimes immensely sad, and that's OK too. Unfortunately, social media trends over the last decade have not helped. In fact, we have moved in the wrong direction. We all see Instagram or Facebook posts of people having idyllic holidays, perfect bodies, and flawless lives. Of course, we know this is not real. But we must change these norms and let our guard down, take off the Instagram façade and talk about what is really going on in our lives and how we feel more often. I am not suggesting we talk about sad and depressing elements of our lives constantly, but I am recommending we do this more frequently and better to reduce the stigma in relation to mental health issues and see that it leads to more understanding and more compassion for those in our society who suffer and struggle the most.

Acknowledgements

This is my second book. Writing the first one was a tremendous learning experience, but creating Compassion required even more help and support from several incredible people. I would like to begin by thanking those who directly contributed to the book's editing and overall development.

I've learned that the first draft of a book is only the beginning. The true work begins when it comes time to refine and perfect. Jaqui Lane from The Book Advisor played a pivotal role in this process, providing invaluable advice and guidance from the outset. While Jaqui was more directly involved with my first book, I reached out to her again when I started Compassion. She read early drafts and helped me shape my ideas. Jaqui suggested changes that significantly enhanced the final version, and I am truly honoured to have her in my corner. She is an incredibly giving person.

Tanya Schiffter, a psychologist who works with me at Steople, also provided crucial feedback. Tanya's insights were especially valuable as I sought another experienced psychologist's perspective. She reviewed Compassion early in its development, offering honest, constructive feedback. Tanya encouraged me to delve deeper into my personal and professional experiences, exploring how they had shaped me. Her suggestions were incredibly insightful and have had a lasting impact on the book.

A long-time friend, Nigel Rose, deserves special recognition. During a coffee chat, I mentioned my work on this book, and he expressed interest in reading it. Nigel could visualize many of the stories and even imagined them as scenes in a movie. He offered to review and edit the stories, ensuring they would paint vivid pictures in the reader's mind. His contributions were invaluable, and I'm grateful for his help in bringing the stories to life.

Once the final draft of Compassion was complete, I needed someone to review, edit, and proofread it. Clare Wadsworth was the perfect person for the job. She was thorough and diligent, correcting grammatical errors and improving the overall readability of the manuscript. Clare's attention to detail helped me polish the book into something I can proudly present to the world. I highly recommend her to anyone seeking expert editing and proofreading services.

Rasika Um played a key role in co-ordinating the book's layout, design, and typesetting, ensuring it was ready for production. Her expertise made the entire process run smoothly.

I am especially grateful to my beautiful daughter, Eliza Fricke, for designing the front and back covers. Creating an image that encapsulated the book's themes of mental illness, sadness, and compassion was no easy task. Eliza's design is a testament to her creativity and talent, and I couldn't be prouder of how she helped bring the book to life in such a meaningful way.

I also received tremendous support from several key people at Steople, the company I founded in 2009 and continue to run. Amy Curran has been with Steople for over 14 years, and her unwavering support has been invaluable. Sarah Merei, who has been with our team for seven years, also contributed greatly to organizing the final stages of the book's production. Both Amy and Sarah played a critical role in ensuring the book's marketing and outreach. Jason Smith, my business partner of nearly 15 years, has been an integral part of this journey. Beyond business, Jason is my best mate—more like a brother—and his support means the world to me.

There are countless details in this book that required accuracy, and I couldn't have remembered everything on my own. I'm deeply thankful to Ian Peter-Budge for his help. Ian and I were close friends when we both embarked on the professional tennis circuit at the age of 18. After nearly 30 years apart, I reached out to Ian for assistance, asking if he could recall details of his trip to Spain with Q when he experienced his first breakdown. Ian's generosity and vivid recollection were essential to accurately portraying this part of the story.

Finally, I must thank my family, whose support has been unwavering throughout this journey. My mother, Judy Carroll, initially hesitated to read Compassion, uncertain if it would be too painful for her. But her courage in reading it and offering her thoughts meant the world to me. We spent hours together discussing her suggestions and reflecting on the book's themes, which proved to be a cathartic experience for both of us. Thank you, Mum.

My sister, Yvette Finemore, went above and beyond in her support. If reading the book was difficult for Mum, it was perhaps even harder for Yvette. As a highly emotional person, she was frequently in tears as we reviewed the stories. Despite the emotional toll, Yvette's dedication to helping me bring the book to completion was remarkable. I am beyond grateful for her support, and I am blessed to have her as my sister.

Although Yvette's daughters and son, Jessica, Georgia and Tim Finemore, contributed to a smaller section towards the back of the book, their input was invaluable. They each showed immense bravery in sharing how their father's story had affected them. Their courage in discussing such difficult subjects is a testament to their strength and resilience. I am incredibly proud of them and honoured to have such powerful young adults as my nieces and nephew.

About Hayden

Hayden Fricke began his adult life as a professional tennis player. However, unlike the glamorous image often associated with the top levels of tennis, Hayden spent most of his time grinding it out on the Satellite Circuit. After a few years, he realized that reaching the top of the sport wasn't in the cards for him. The underlying challenge was his own struggle to cope with the anxiety, stress, and pressure of high-level competition and life on tour—an issue that was never addressed or discussed with him. It was this realization that sparked his interest in Sport Psychology, and he soon discovered that this was his true passion.

At the same time, Hayden was navigating significant family trauma. His younger brother experienced a mental breakdown and was later diagnosed with schizophrenia, while his older brother, who had an intellectual disability, battled anxiety and depression. To add to the emotional strain, his parents went through a difficult divorce. Hayden wanted to help but didn't know how. His desire to understand human behaviour, both for himself and his family, led him to pursue a career in psychology. This journey began over 30 years ago.

Hayden attended university and became a psychologist, working in various fields, including sport psychology, drug and alcohol counselling, and mental health. His initial aim was to build his practice in sport psychology. However, his true passion lay in positive psychology, which led him to pursue a Master's degree in Organisational Psychology in 1996. He has been working in this field ever since.

For about 15 years, Hayden held various senior roles, including Consulting Organisational Psychologist for a global consulting firm, Director of People and Culture for a Melbourne-based financial services company, General Manager of a large business in the financial services sector, and Group Head of Organisational Development for a major global business in the property, facility, and catering sector. These experiences proved invaluable when Hayden founded Steople in 2009.

Together with a remarkable team of Directors, Hayden has built Steople into a highly successful global consulting firm, with offices in Australia, New Zealand, and the USA. His vision is to create a legacy that extends beyond his own lifetime, by developing a community of people committed to creating great places to work across the globe. Steople is a key part of this legacy, as is his first book, Leaders, Do You Have Your Sh*t Together?, which embodies his commitment to leadership and workplace culture.

His second book, Compassion, is a much more personal reflection on his journey with a family grappling with mental health issues. Along with his sister, Hayden has spent countless hours supporting his brother Craig, who has faced many difficult challenges in his life.

Outside of work, Hayden still plays and enjoys tennis, along with a variety of other activities to stay fit and healthy, such as biking, swimming, gym workouts, skiing, surfing, and walking. He is deeply grateful for his family, which includes his wife Lynne and their three inspiring young adult children: Eliza, Josh, and Jemma.

© 2025 Hayden Fricke
Website: www.steople.com.au
For bulk copies please contact: info@steople.com.au

All rights reserved. No part of this publication may be reproduced, stored in a retrieval system, or transmitted in any form or by means, electronic, mechanical, photocopying, recording or otherwise without prior written permission of the publisher and copyright holders.

The authors assert the moral right to be identified as the authors of this work.

A catalogue record for this book is available from the National Library of Australia.

Printed book ISBN: 978-06-46715-53-7

Disclaimer: The material in this publication is intended to provide general information and comment only, and does not represent professional advice. It is not intended to provide specific guidance for particular circumstances and it should not be relied on as the basis for any decision to take action or not take action on any matter which it covers. Readers should obtain professional advice, where appropriate before making any such decision or utilising and products or services mentioned.

This information is provided for persons in Australia only and is not provided for the use of anyone who is in another country. To the maximum extent permitted by law, the authors and the publisher disclaim all responsibility and liability to any person, whether a purchaser of this publication or not, arising directly or indirectly from any person taking or not taking action based on the information in the publication.

Every effort has been made by the author to trace and acknowledge copyright material. The publisher would be pleased to hear from any copyright holders who have not been acknowledged.

Cover Design: Eliza Fricke
Proofreader: Clare Wadsworth
Internal page design: Rasika UM, www.shashika.info
Printed in Australia by PeopleScape (VIC) Pty Ltd